HeadSt[illegible]
prim

English Reading Comprehension

Success in Year 6

Written and illustrated
by Jim Edmiston

HeadStart
primary

Acknowledgements:

Author: Jim Edmiston

Cover and Page Design: Jim Edmiston and Kathryn Webster

HeadStart primary

HeadStart Primary Ltd
Elker Lane
Clitheroe
BB7 9HZ

T. 01200 423405
E. info@headstartprimary.com
www.headstartprimary.com

Published by HeadStart Primary Ltd © **HeadStart Primary Ltd**

A record for this book is available from the British Library -
ISBN: 978-1-908767-37-0

HeadStart
primary

Year 6

CONTENTS

INTRODUCTION

HeadStart Primary English Reading Comprehension has been produced to make the teacher's formative assessment of reading as straightforward as possible. At the same time, its aim is to develop children's reading skills and encourage their engagement with literature in all its forms.

With this in mind, sections have been organised to follow closely the National Curriculum and the different reading skills (content domains) highlighted in the KS2 English Reading Test Framework 2016 (available to download at www.gov.uk), with an emphasis on **comprehension, making inferences, language for effect** and **themes and conventions**.

The tasks presented here increase in difficulty as you work through a section. This allows for:

- easier access for the child still acquiring and developing basic skills
- a challenge for the child whose skills are more secure
- a further challenge and consolidation for the child who is in the process of exceeding year group expectations.

This will enable the teacher to monitor the progress a child is making in each particular skill area, thereby easing the process of formative assessment and subsequent planning. An individual child, for instance, may have a wide vocabulary but lack inferential skills. The organisation of tasks will make this apparent so that the child's learning can be moved forward.

A range of fiction and non-fiction underpins the reading tasks as well as the range of texts in the **TESTS** section. Since the removal of national curriculum levels, schools are now free to choose their own methods of monitoring progress in reading. The tests here have been provided to help the process of formative assessment, but they could be used simply to give children experience of the test format. This is for the professional judgement of the class teacher. It is worth noting that, where a school is using the tests to monitor progress year by year, the tests provided here do, in fact, offer coverage of the different reading skills comparable to the SATs tests. This means the highest percentage of questions relate to domains 2b (retrieving information) and 2d (making and justifying inferences), followed by 2a (words in context), 2c (summarising main ideas), followed by the other domains.

Finally, the texts have been chosen in relation to Year 6 subject areas, their age-appropriate spelling lists and with the enjoyment of reading in mind.

Words in context

Strand: Comprehension

National Curriculum reference:

- checking that the text makes sense to them

Reading Test / Content Domain links: 2a, 2b

I KNOW WHAT YOU MEAN

Some words have the same spelling (homographs) but mean different things. This shows you how much we rely on the rest of the sentence (context) to tell us what such words mean. Use the context of the following sentences to choose the correct meaning of the words in **bold**. Put a tick in the circle.

1. The rock star walked to the microphone and began to **address** the audience.
   - write the destination on a parcel ○
   - give a speech ○ ✓

2. In the word 'beginning', the **stress** is on the second syllable.
   - emphasis ○ ✓
   - physical force ○
   - emotional strain ○

3. The witch was able to cast a spell to **entrance** her victims.
   - the moment an actor comes on stage ○
   - enchant ○ ✓
   - doorway ○

4. To **conduct** a large orchestra takes years of practice.
   - personal behaviour ○
   - guide ○ ✓
   - channel heat or electricity ○

5. America and the UK came to a military **compact** during the war.
   - small make-up case ○
   - packed together ○ ✓
   - formal agreement ○

Read extract and the words + start, move on if stuck. Work out by the context and by elimination. Needed help, well done.

ON THE RUN

Chase scenes are common in novels and films. In this description, a number of key words are missing. Fill in the blanks using the list of words provided. Use the context of each sentence as a guide.

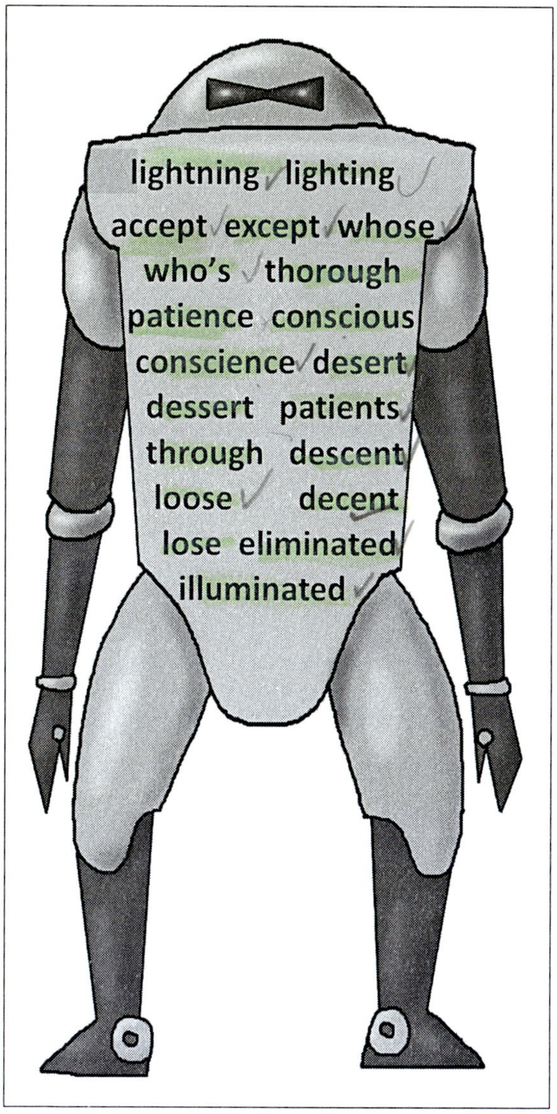

The lighting is so poor in the back streets in the dead of night, that it takes a jagged knife of lightning to streak across the sky before I can see the way ahead. I have to accept the fact that no one dares step outside except me. So who's going to know or care whose car this is? The police will surely lose patience if I try to tell them there is a killer robot on the loose. I could easily end up as one of the Patients in the local hospital for disturbed personalities! Anyway, I'm only too conscious of the fact that it's me that thing is after, and, in all conscience I can't let it wreak havoc in my city. No time to hang around and become some kind of robot desert. Heading out to the dessert is my one chance. Throught the suburbs, out past the city limits and be as thorough as I can in planning my next move. Put a decent mileage between me and it before that final descent down into Death Valley. Illuminated by the stars, the dirt road snakes away into the unknown – my only hope of not being eliminated.

TRACK DOWN THE SYNONYMS

Here are pages from the notebook of a wildlife photographer on a lonely moor.

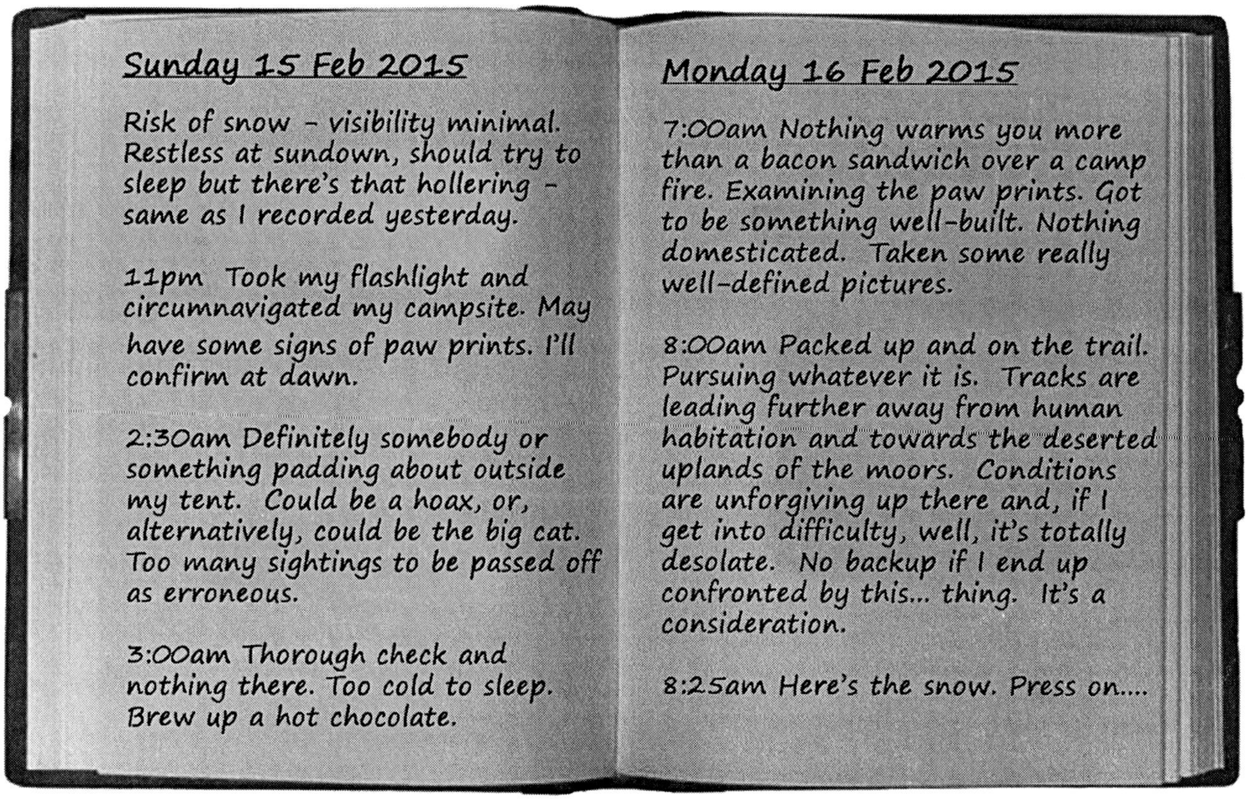

Sunday 15 Feb 2015

Risk of snow - visibility minimal. Restless at sundown, should try to sleep but there's that hollering - same as I recorded yesterday.

11pm Took my flashlight and circumnavigated my campsite. May have some signs of paw prints. I'll confirm at dawn.

2:30am Definitely somebody or something padding about outside my tent. Could be a hoax, or, alternatively, could be the big cat. Too many sightings to be passed off as erroneous.

3:00am Thorough check and nothing there. Too cold to sleep. Brew up a hot chocolate.

Monday 16 Feb 2015

7:00am Nothing warms you more than a bacon sandwich over a camp fire. Examining the paw prints. Got to be something well-built. Nothing domesticated. Taken some really well-defined pictures.

8:00am Packed up and on the trail. Pursuing whatever it is. Tracks are leading further away from human habitation and towards the deserted uplands of the moors. Conditions are unforgiving up there and, if I get into difficulty, well, it's totally desolate. No backup if I end up confronted by this... thing. It's a consideration.

8:25am Here's the snow. Press on....

Find synonyms (words that mean the same or are similar) for the following:

word	synonym	word	synonym
danger		muscular	
fidgety		tame	
howling		clear	
taped		following	
torch		settlement	
moved around		hills	
double check		harsh	
practical joke		bleak	
on the other hand		support	
mistaken		face to face	
inspecting		thought	

WORD ASSOCIATION

There are some words that you might expect to see in the same context – in the same place at the same time. Draw lines connecting those words that are, in some way, linked to each other. One has already been done for you.

bargain	gymnastics
occupation	artefact
restaurant	parliament
accident	discount
government	community
ancient	meaning
neighbour	message
dictionary	dessert
competition	salary
communicate	disaster

HOLIDAY TALK

This is the way holidays aboard cruise ships are often described in brochures.

Stepping aboard the stylish Southern Star is like walking into a stunning hotel with its innovative approach to exploring the best the world has to give. Your tour will encompass the beautiful wall-paintings and artefacts of ancient and vibrant civilisations, as well as the colour of the bazaars that have bewitched travellers for centuries. Relax as we traverse the shimmering blue waters of the Mediterranean or idle away an hour in the mesmerising infinity pool on Deck 6. On the third day, you will awake to the cultural charm of the most opulent palace on one of the most unspoiled islands anywhere in the world. Here, 16th Century opulence meets 21st Century modernity – a fascinating fusion of old and new. We wait to welcome you on board.

Find words that mean the same as, or are similar in meaning, to the following:

hypnotic ____________________

breathtaking ____________________

entranced ____________________

include ____________________

luxurious ____________________

art objects ____________________

sparkling ____________________

mixture ____________________

lively ____________________

new ____________________

THE SCIENCE LESSON

Read what Josh has to say about his day at school, then answer the questions about the meanings of some of the words he uses.

Usually, when Mum or Dad ask me how school was, I just shrug and head for the fridge. But yesterday, I thought I'd surprise them. I said we'd been working with man-made materials as well as natural ones. Plastic, for instance, is synthetic, but wood just... like... grows on trees. We were investigating their properties: whether you could see through them or not, or whether they were opaque. Some materials bend easily; others aren't so flexible. Some metals are quite malleable; other things snap in two if you try to bend them. I opened the chocolate biscuits, you know, to demonstrate. I said I hope they had been paying attention, because I would be making them do a quiz later.

Now for Mum and Dad's quiz. Find the words that have the following meanings:

1. The opposite of transparent. ____________________
2. The features or qualities of a material. ____________________
3. Two words that mean: not found in nature. ____________________

   ____
4. Two words that mean: easily bent. ____________________

   ____
5. To show that something is true. ____________________
6. Exploring and researching. ____________________

THE CASE OF THE KIDNAPPED CAMELOPARD

A certain Victorian detective is called upon to solve another case. Here he talks about it using English words that are no longer in use. Perhaps you can detect what he means.

The Case of the Kidnapped Camelopard

Having been burdened of late – a full sennight – by a bout of the ague, I was in no measure up to snuff and prepared for another criminal case so soon. But there was the headline: 'Camelopard Kidnapped From Circus'. Ere rapping at my good friend, Witson's, door – the man's no mooncalf, if something of a slugabed – I hied to the apothecary, Mr Jackson.

His premises, I have to say, are an assault on the senses, with countless grimalkins and popinjays. Even the man's walls are festooned with fandangles. You must understand that I was not after any of his foul banes. My landlady insists that a daily serving of one of her hotchpotches will cure all. And, by Jiminy, she's right! No, the man is a quidnunc of the highest order and knows every detail of the city's darker goings-on.

Passing God's acre, I had the misfortune to bump into the one and only (thank Zeus!) Snivelling Sid: a rapscallion at best, but also a cutpurse straight out of bridewell. I ought to know since I was the one to hand him over to the turnkeys. He bore me no malice. On the contrary, well out of sight of nearby peelers, on the pretext of asking me for a Lucifer, he passed me a bodkin, warning of the criminal company kept by my apothecary acquaintance lately, and the amount of pelf in his deep pockets nowadays.

Sid doffed his cap and sauntered into the church, promising to say an orison for me. I thanked old Sid for both bodkin and orison and thought better of using Jackson's front door.

The courtyard at the rear of the building proved to be quite a revelation. Here, in fact, was the kidnapped camelopard! Will a peterman stop at nothing these days? Jackson could hardly deny it, threw himself at my feet like the poltroon he is, and begged me to save him from the nubbing-cheat. As it turned out, who should drop by but my excellent friend, Witson, out to purchase some sugarplums for me. Needless to say, the dorbies he always carries about his person came in rather handy. Case solved.

Here are a list of possible words to help you translate the detective's account into modern-day English. (Put your new words inside the brackets.) There are a few red-herrings in there, so be careful.

dagger	cats	police officers	pickpocket	tiger	poisons	malaria	fool
parrots	baker	raised	mutton stews	churchyard	chemist	library	giraffe
handcuffs	standard	week	lazy person	pirate	boiled sweets	camel	
reform school	hospital	match	money	coward	went quickly	thief	
ornaments	before	jailers	prayer	mischievous person	gossip	gallows	

Having been burdened of late – a full **sennight** ( ) – by a bout of the **ague** ( ), I was in no measure up to **snuff** ( ) and prepared for another criminal case so soon. But there was the headline: '**Camelopard** ( )Kidnapped From Circus'. **Ere** ( ) rapping at my good friend, Witson's, door – the man's no **mooncalf** ( ), if something of a **slugabed** ( ) – I **hied** ( ) to the **apothecary** ( ), Mr Jackson.

His premises, I have to say, are an assault on the senses, with countless **grimalkins** ( ) and **popinjays** ( ). Even the man's walls are festooned with **fandangles** ( ). You must understand that I was not after any of his foul **banes** ( ). My landlady insists that a daily serving of one of her **hotchpotches** ( ) will cure all. And, by Jiminy, she's right! No, the man is a **quidnunc** ( ) of the highest order and knows every detail of the city's darker goings-on.

Passing **God's acre** ( ), I had the misfortune to bump into the one and only (thank Zeus!) Snivelling Sid: a **rapscallion** ( ) at best, but also a **cutpurse** ( )

straight out of **bridewell** ( ). I ought to know since I was the one to hand him over to the **turnkeys** ( ). He bore me no malice. On the contrary, well out of sight of nearby **peelers**, ( ) on the pretext of asking me for a **Lucifer** ( ), he passed me a **bodkin** ( ), warning of the criminal company kept by my **apothecary** ( )acquaintance lately, and the amount of **pelf** ( ) in his deep pockets nowadays.

Sid **doffed** ( ) his cap and sauntered into the church, promising to say an **orison** ( ) for me. I thanked old Sid for both **bodkin** ( ) and **orison** ( ) and thought better of using Jackson's front door.

The courtyard at the rear of the building proved to be quite a revelation. Here, in fact, was the kidnapped **camelopard** ( )! Will a **peterman** ( ) stop at nothing these days? Jackson could hardly deny it, threw himself at my feet like the **poltroon** ( ) he is, and begged me to save him from the **nubbing-cheat** ( ). As it turned out, who should drop by but my excellent friend, Witson, out to purchase some **sugarplums** ( ) for me. Needless to say, the **darbies** ( ) he always carries about his person came in rather handy. Case solved.

Explaining words in context

Strand: Comprehension

National Curriculum reference:

- [checking that the text makes sense to them], discussing their understanding, and explaining the meaning of words in context

Reading Test / Content Domain links: 2a, 2b, 2f

VEXING VOCABULARY

Context helps when you're trying to work out the meaning of a word. Tick the correct meaning of the words in **bold**, then explain your choice. One has been done already.

1. He might look **culpable**, but we have no evidence.

blameworthy	☑
dangerous	☐
lonely	☐

Explanation: 'but we have no evidence' suggests someone is to **blame** for a crime.

2. We don't know who left the gate open but James looks **sheepish**.

woolly	☐
guilty	☐
tired	☐

Explanation: ______________________________

3. With the new training in place, Chen is very **bullish** about the team's future.

upbeat	☐
overweight	☐
pessimistic	☐

Explanation: ______________________________

4. Jamila's plan to tightrope-walk across the ravine is quite **audacious**.

foolish	☐
ingenious	☐
bold	☐

Explanation: ______________________________

5. Kazuo felt **exasperated** after spending an hour trying to thread the needle.

relieved	☐
frustrated	☐
breathless	☐

Explanation: ______________________________

6. Rolling the boulder uphill was an **arduous** task.

unfortunate ☐

backbreaking ☐

long-winded ☐

Explanation: ______________________________
____
____
____

7. Having done no revision for her exams, Marjory felt quite **apprehensive**.

anxious ☐

confident ☐

courageous ☐

Explanation: ______________________________
____
____
____

8. It was **inconsiderate** of Catriona to leave the new girl out of the team.

understandable ☐

thoughtless ☐

generous ☐

Explanation: ______________________________
____
____
____

9. Luckily, Jasper faced a **compassionate** judge who let him off with a warning.

kind-hearted ☐

pitiless ☐

overworked ☐

Explanation: ______________________________
____
____
____

10. **Clandestine** meetings of the stamp-collecting group were held in the cellar.

fortnightly ☐

regular ☐

undercover ☐

Explanation: ______________________________
____
____
____

USING THE WRONG ~~WORMS~~ (WORDS)

When you use the wrong word in place of one that sounds similar, it's called a **malapropism** after a character – Mrs Malaprop – who did this a lot in a play called 'The Rivals'. Pick out the wrong word in these sentences and explain why it is wrong.

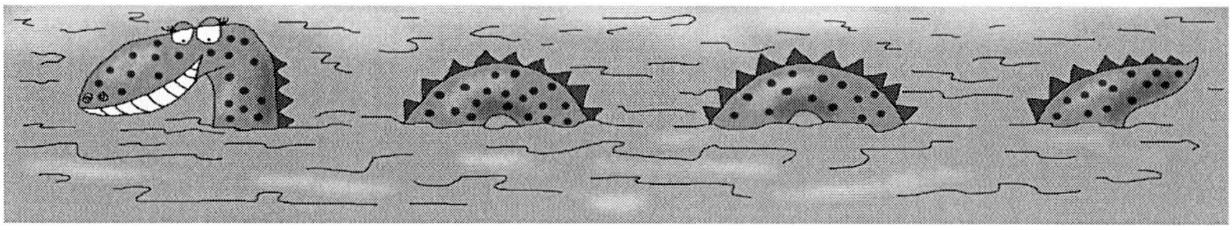

"A, e, i, o, u – nobody can say I don't know my bowels."

____________________ **because it should be** ____________________

"What would help trees grow in the Sahara Desert is a bit more irritation."

____________________ **because it should be** ____________________

"It's like an Aladdin's cave in that second-hand shop: full of wonderful antics."

____________________ **because it should be** ____________________

"Well, when I got my test results, you could have knocked me over with a ferret."

____________________ **because it should be** ____________________

"The flooding in Somerset was so bad they had to evaporate the villages."

____________________ **because it should be** ____________________

"The Loch Ness Monster is just an optical conclusion, or else a pigment of your imagination."

____________________ **because it should be** ____________________

____________________ **because it should be** ____________________

"If there's a hole in the boat, then it's lost its porpoise."

____________________ **because it should be** ____________________

"Some of the pheasants in medieval times had quite cruel masters."

____________________ **because it should be** ____________________

"I'm a doctor, so when I saw the woman faint, I bent down and took her purse."

______________________ **because it should be**______________________________

"It must have been awful in the 17th century with all that blue bonnet plague."

______________________ **because it should be**______________________________

"If I run away to the circus, I'm going to be a jugular."

______________________ **because it should be**______________________________

"The shoplifter tried to run out of the store but got stuck in the revolting doors."

______________________ **because it should be**______________________________

"A triangle has three angels, and the one with three equal sides is equatorial."

______________________ **because it should be**______________________________

______________________ **because it should be**______________________________

"The king looked very splendid in a purple cape edged with vermin."

______________________ **because it should be**______________________________

"I decided I'd be better at painting portraits if I bought myself a new weasel."

______________________ **because it should be**______________________________

"I'd never have survived the sweltering dessert without the help of my caramel."

______________________ **because it should be**______________________________

______________________ **because it should be**______________________________

"I spent some time at university doing a hysterical study of the Tudors."

______________________ **because it should be**______________________________

"I got so fed up of gardening, I decided to cover the whole area in grovel."

______________________ **because it should be**______________________________

Retrieving and recording information

Strand: Comprehension

National Curriculum reference:

- retrieving and recording information / identifying key details from fiction and non-fiction

Reading Test / Content Domain links: 2a, 2b

THE RAILWAY AGE

This group of children have been working on the coming of the railways. Each one gives a short presentation to the class.

The start of the railway age is accepted as 1825 when the Stockton-Darlington line was opened, first for coal wagons and then passengers.

When the railways arrived people travelled faster and further. The journey from London to Edinburgh took 30 hours less than by coach.

Improved transport meant raw materials such as coal and iron could be delivered faster and more cheaply. Farm machinery, for example, cost less, which led to cheaper food.

The delivery of newspapers from London and mail up and down the country was more efficient. More interest was taken in what was happening nationally and in the laws being passed by government.

Because the prices of food and other goods came down, demand for them increased. This meant more people were employed on the land and in factories.

Rail tracks and stations, and railway engineering towns, such as Crewe, York and Doncaster, changed the landscape. People used this cheaper mode of travel to enjoy leisure time. As a result, seaside towns welcomed day trippers.

The success of Stephenson's steam engine, 'Rocket' in 1829 (it could go 30mph), led to 'Railway Mania' and many new railway lines were built.

By 1900, Britain had 22,000 miles of rail track constructed by men known as 'navvies'.

In 1841, Isambard Kingdom Brunel completed the line from London to Bristol. Since it was called the Great Western Railway – GWR – people referred to it as 'God's Wonderful Railway'.

1. What was the route of the first railway line that opened?

2. Describe **two** ways in which the landscape was changed.

3. What invention inspired 'Railway Mania'?

4. How did rail travel compare with travel by coach?

5. What was the nickname given to the men who laid the railway track?

6. Who was the engineer who created God's Wonderful Railway?

7. Complete the following table by describing how the railways changed different aspects of life in Victorian Britain:

aspect	influence of the railways
food	
employment	
government	

WEB-LINKS: SPIDERS

Read this information about spiders, then decide whether the statements that follow are **true** or **false**.

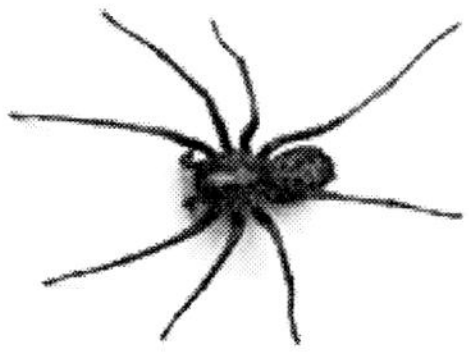

General Characteristics

Spiders, scorpions, mites and ticks are all part of a large group of animals called 'arachnids'. Unlike insects, which have three body parts, spiders have two, have no wings or antennae, and have eight legs and forty-eight knees. There are almost 40,000 different species of spider in the world, the biggest being the Goliath Tarantula which can catch birds.

Other Physical Features

Unlike vertebrates, spiders do not have a skeleton inside their bodies. Instead, they have a hard outer shell known as an 'exoskeleton'. This cannot grow as the young spider gets bigger; so it has to be shed by a process called 'moulting'. The spider crawls out and waits, in a vulnerable state, while its new outer protection hardens.

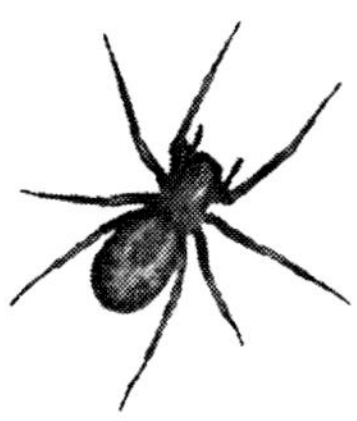

Wolf Spiders

Wolf spiders don't spin webs. They are lone hunters with excellent eyesight, two of its eight eyes being quite large.

Food

Spiders are carnivorous. Some will eat other spiders. Their legs are covered in hairs which pick up vibrations and smells of possible prey nearby. Having small mouths, they inject poison into their captives with their sharp fangs. This poison 'digests' the victim, turning their insides into a kind of soup, which the spider then feeds on.

Spiders' Webs

At the back of the spider's body are 'spinnerets', which, when pressed against an object, force out some silk in liquid form. As the spider moves to another place, the liquid is drawn out and then hardens in the air. It doesn't stick to its own web because of an oily substance it spreads on to its feet.

Now decide whether the following statements are **true** or **false** and **tick** the appropriate boxes.

statement	true	false
Spiders are eight-legged insects.		
Ants are a type of arachnid.		
Spiders have two body parts.		
There are more than 40,000 different species of spider on Earth.		
Vertebrates have a hard skeleton inside their bodies.		
The exoskeleton of a spider grows as it gets bigger.		
A spider has little protection the moment it crawls out of its exoskeleton.		
A spider can smell with its legs.		
Spiders kills their prey with sharp fangs that inject poison.		
A spider's web silk starts off in liquid form.		
The spider uses an oily substance to harden the silk threads for its web.		
Spiders are forever getting stuck in their own webs.		
All spiders spin webs.		
Wolf spiders hunt in packs like wolves.		

HOWARD CARTER – BIOGRAPHY OF AN ARCHAEOLOGIST

Here are some biographical details of the archaeologist, Howard Carter, who famously discovered the tomb of Tutankhamun.

Howard Carter and the Curse of the Pharaohs

Howard Carter (9 May 1874 – 2 March 1939) was an English archaeologist and Egyptologist who gained world fame after discovering the intact tomb of 14th century BC pharaoh, Tutankhamun, in November 1922.

Born in Kensington, London, son of Samuel Carter, an artist, the young Howard was encouraged to develop his artistic talents. In 1891, the Egypt Exploration Fund, very impressed by his recording and classifying skills, sent him to participate in the excavation of Middle Kingdom tombs. (Although only 17, Carter was innovative in improving the methods of copying tomb decoration.)

Detail of wall painting - Temple of Hatshepsut

Between 1892 and 1899 he gained much hands-on experience working with various established archaeologists. At Deir el-Bahari, adjacent to the Valley of the Kings, he recorded the wall reliefs in the Temple of Hatshepsut.

In 1899, Carter began supervising a number of excavations at Thebes (now known as Luxor). His reputation grew, and, in 1907, Lord Carnarvon asked him to supervise Carnarvon's Egyptian excavations in the Valley of the Kings. After several years of finding little, Lord Carnarvon, concerned about the cost of funding the project, became dissatisfied with the lack of results. In 1922, he informed Carter that he had one more season left.

On 4 November 1922, Howard Carter's excavation group found steps which Carter hoped led to a tomb. On Carnarvon's arrival on 26 November 1922, Carter breached the doorway using the chisel his grandmother had given him on his 17th birthday. Inside, were the untouched treasures of Tutankhamun, the boy king.

Newspapers at the time made exaggerated claims about the 'curse of the pharaohs'. Within six months, Lord Carnarvon and his dog were dead ... of natural causes. Howard Carter, however, lived another seventeen years and died aged 64. Despite reports, one item not found in the tomb was any inscription which said:

CURSED BE THOSE THAT DISTURB THE REST OF PHARAOH!

1. What was it that brought Howard Carter to the public's attention?

____

____

2. Part of his upbringing helped him in his adult work. What was that and how did it help him?

____

____

3. What helped him improve as an archaeologist between 1892 and 1899?

____

4. The text gives an example of Carter's drawing skills. What was that?

____

____

5. What is the modern name for the old Egyptian capital of Thebes?

____

6. Which area of Egypt was Lord Carnarvon interested in excavating?

____

7. Why did Lord Carnarvon ask Carter to supervise the work?

____

8. Why was the project under threat by 1922?

____

9. What single piece of evidence suggests that no curse existed?

____

____

THE INDUS VALLEY

Read this information about the civilisation that grew up in the valley of the River Indus around 3000 BC, then answer the follow-up questions.

Mohenjo-Daro

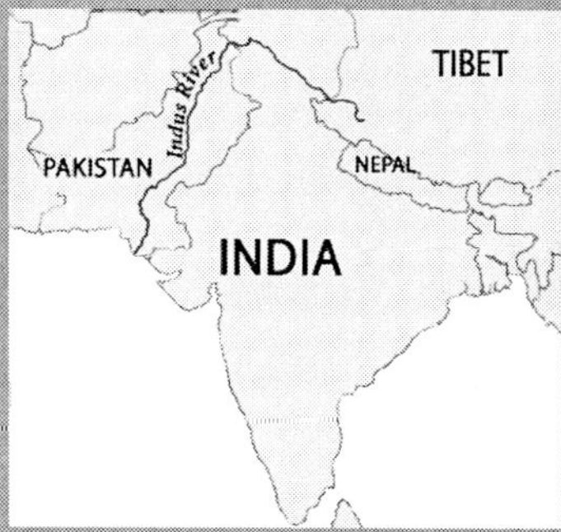

The Indus River flows almost 2000 miles from its source in Tibet in the Himalayas through modern-day Pakistan and Northern India to the Indian Ocean.

About ninety years ago, archaeologists began to excavate the ancient site of Mohenjo-Daro, translated as 'Mound of the Dead', which was built around 2500 BC and flourished in the Indus Valley.

We think of urban planning as a modern concept, but it existed here in the form of strong city walls containing a network of streets, the world's earliest example of sanitation, granaries for storing food, wells to supply water and bathing rooms. Houses had separate living and sleeping areas and were built with upstairs rooms and courtyards.

Unearthed seals, such as this example, showing a bull or possibly a unicorn, were carved out of stone, and, as a result of their durability, have told archaeologists a lot about this early civilisation. They appear to have been pressed into clay to create tags, similar to a label, for traded goods.

Seals typically have an image of an animal with an example of the script of the Indus Valley language along the top. Markings like these have been found on other objects, showing that people wrote the first line from right to left, the second line from left to right, and so on. Altogether, four hundred separate symbols have been found, but, as yet, no one has successfully deciphered them. Possibly, the inscriptions are a record of some business agreement or the identity of the supplier.

1. In the 1st paragraph, why might the writer have used the phrase **modern-day** to describe Pakistan?

____

2. In the 2nd paragraph, which word suggests this civilisation was very successful?

____

3. What archaeological evidence is there that the layout of Mohenjo-Daro was planned before it was built?

____

4. Why might the urban planning of the city be a surprise to us?

____

____

5. Why do you think it was possible to have bathing rooms and sanitation?

____

____

6. What does **unearthed** mean?

____

7. The seals were carved out of stone. Why would an archaeologist find this useful?

____

____

8. What evidence has been found to prove how the seals were used?

____

____

9. Why has the writer used the word **typically** when describing the seals?

____

____

10. In the last paragraph, four different words are used to refer to the letters in the Indus Valley language. What are they?

____

____

____

____

11. Find the phrase or sentence that points out that we are still not sure what the symbols mean.

____

12. Write down two words or phrases that suggest archaeologists are careful to avoid making claims that cannot be supported by evidence.

____

____

13. How do the two images support the text?

____

____

____

EMMELINE PANKHURST

Read this information about Emmeline Pankhurst and answer the questions that follow.

Emmeline Pankhurst

Born on the 15th July 1858 in Manchester to a family in which political discussions were commonplace, Emmeline Goulden was unquestionably one of the most influential figures of the 20th century.

In 1879, she married Richard Pankhurst, a lawyer and supporter of the women's suffrage movement, i.e. the right of women to have the vote. His death in 1898 was a great shock to Emmeline.

In 1888, she supported a strike involving the women who worked at the Bryant and May matches factory, where women worked fourteen hours a day and were fined if they dropped matches on the floor. At about the same time, she was also concerned about conditions in Manchester's workhouses, where poor people without work were confined – sometimes in inhuman conditions. Her meetings, held in local parks to draw the public's attention to what was going on, were declared illegal.

In 1903, she helped to create the Women's Social and Political Union (WSPU). Her daughters, Christabel and Sylvia, were also active members. This organisation would soon gain notoriety for its headline-grabbing activities: politicians and the general public were often shocked when they smashed windows, tied themselves to railings outside Parliament, and were involved in arson attacks. In 1913, Emily Davison, a WSPU member, was killed when, in protest against the government's unfair treatment of women, she threw herself in front of the King George V's racehorse at the Epsom Derby.

It was during this period that Emmeline Pankhurst and her followers were nicknamed the 'suffragettes'.

It was common for suffragettes to be arrested. In prison they would go on a hunger strike, which led to force feeding. This prompted the government to pass what was dubbed the 'Cat and Mouse' Act – a law that allowed hunger-striking prisoners to be released and then re-arrested once they grew healthy and strong again.

In 1914, on the declaration of war, Emmeline turned her energy to helping with the war effort. In 1918, voting rights were given to women over the age of thirty. Emmeline died on 14th June 1928 not long after a law was passed granting women equal voting rights with men.

1. What **two** early influences helped to form Emmeline Pankhurst's views about women's rights?

2. What major change happened in Emmeline's life in 1898?

3. In 1886, what were employment conditions like for Bryant and May workers ?

4. At this time, what other issue did Mrs Pankhurst involve herself in?

5. What sorts of activities of the WSPU hit the headlines?

6. What dramatic event took place at the Epsom Derby?

7. What was the nickname that Mrs Pankhurst and her followers were given?

8. Explain what was meant by the 'Cat and Mouse' Act.

9. When did women over the age of thirty get the vote?

THE LIFE OF A FOREST

Here is a range of information about forests and the part they play in our environment.

THE BIRTH OF A FOREST

Barren rock is colonised by lichens and moss

Ferns and small plants take root in soil

Larger shrubs and small trees begin to dominate

Mature forest with tree canopy and understorey

A BALANCED SYSTEM

Ancient woods with their varied mix of trees and plant life provide a whole range of wild mammals, birds and insects with a delicate eco-system, their lives in a state of balance. It is possible that seed-loving birds, squirrels and mice could, in theory, eat all the seeds of the next generation of trees, but it's unlikely. In any case, these animals are, themselves, the food of predators, such as owls and foxes. If the predators are too successful, they will decline in numbers because of lack of food. In this way, plants and animals depend on each other for their survival. In creating the right environment, they are the environment.

THE FOREST ABLAZE

Long before human beings came along, fires caused naturally by lightning and, rarely, by volcanic activity, were part of the cycle of destruction and renewal of woodland. The risks have increased with the introduction of timber-cutting machinery, campfires and the careless discarding of matches. The carbon content of living trees as well as brushwood and leaf litter at ground level provide a vast supply of fuel for wildfire. The destruction of wildlife and the threat to adjacent human habitation can be immense. Tackling such infernos is like a military operation with an almost equal risk to the lives of fire-fighters.

FOREST FOLKLORE

The **rowan** tree was once used as a charm against witchcraft. On the Isle of Man, rowan crosses, made without a knife are tied to the tails of cows to protect them from evil. Wood from the **ash** tree was used to cure warts. To bring **hawthorn** blossom inside was thought to foretell a death in the family. **Yew** trees are often found in graveyards because, being evergreen, they symbolise the possibility of everlasting life. **Willow** has traditionally been used to cure the sick. (Its bark contains the basic ingredient of aspirin.)

1. What phrase in **The Birth of a Forest** refers to branches and leaves at different levels?

____

2. Describe the kind of habitat an old forest provides.

____

3. What part do predators play in ensuring the continuation of the next generation of trees?

____

____

4. What would happen if owls and foxes were too successful?

____

____

5. Before human beings evolved, what two natural phenomena caused forest fires?

____

____

6. Name **three** human activities which have increased the threat of fire.

____

____

____

7. Once a blaze establishes itself, how does the forest, itself, provide fuel?

____

____

8. How might people be in danger from forest fires?

____

____

9. What is the simile that is used to describe the work of fire-fighters?

____

10. Where might you find cows being protected from evil?

____

11. If you were a believer in ancient folklore, why might you be wary of hawthorn?

____

12. Why was the yew tree associated with everlasting life?

____

13. **(Its bark contains the basic ingredient of aspirin.)** Why has the writer placed this sentence inside brackets?

____

____

14. Find two words or phrases that have been used instead of **forest**.

____

____

15. In **The Forest Ablaze**, find two words that are used instead of fire.

____

____

Fact and opinion

Strand: Comprehension

National Curriculum reference:

- retrieving and recording information from non-fiction
- distinguishing between statements of fact and opinion

Reading Test / Content Domain links: 2a, 2b, 2g

PLUTO AND NEW HORIZONS

Scientists try to be very precise. Their training teaches them to make **formal** statements that can be verified by evidence. Of course, they are also human and when the space probe, New Horizons, launched in January 2006, flew past Pluto and successfully sent home lots of information, scientists, in their excitement, made a few **informal** remarks as well. Write **formal** or **informal** after each statement.

Pluto and its large moon, Charon, are 5 billion km from the Sun in the dim outskirts of the Solar System. ____________________

Data from New Horizons will downlink to Earth over the next sixteen months. ____________________

This observation is so tantalising, I'm finding it hard to patiently wait for more data to arrive. ____________________

Pluto's surface, including the distinctive heart-shaped area, is covered by several different types of ice. ____________________

Pluto is a really fascinating place – both beautiful and strange. ____________________

I knew it was going to be cool. I just didn't know it was going to be this cool. ____________________

THE ECCENTRIC ARTIST

Read this information about an American artist. It contains **facts** and **opinions**. Then **tick** the correct boxes.

Walter Anderson was born in New Orleans on 29 September 1903 and died in the same city on the coast of Mississippi on 30 November 1965. It was in Ocean Springs that the family opened Shearwater Pottery – still operating today – selling ceramics, paintings and woodcarvings. Managed by his older brother, Peter, it may have been the case that Walter, an emerging artist, found this highly frustrating. He referred to his work on small, decorated figures sold to the tourist trade as the manufacture of 'widgets'.

His frustrations, the death of his father, and recurring bouts of malaria and fever possibly led to depression and a mental breakdown. No one can be sure. Between 1938 and 1940, he spent some time in and out of mental hospitals. It has been said that, on one occasion, he escaped by tying sheets together and climbing out of the window.

He spent his later years hidden away in a wooded corner of Shearwater inside a wooden shack which he kept padlocked. He must have been a lonely man. When he died and family members entered his sanctuary, they must have been amazed. Every inch of every wall and ceiling is painted in bright, jewel-like colours. The creatures of the coast – butterflies, crickets, deer, possum, blue jays, fish, frogs, lizards and alligators – are displayed in their habitats of entangled branches, flowers and rivers. Today, the sight is still breathtaking.

Few visitors to Shearwater today are allowed access to the simple shack that is, in effect, a shrine to the work of this artist. No doubt, many would love to see inside. For there, it still stands, a doorway to the creative mind of Walter Anderson.

Now decide whether the following statements are **facts** or **opinions**.

statement	fact	opinion
Walter Anderson was born in New Orleans.		
Shearwater Pottery is still operating today.		
Walter found decorating figures for the tourist trade highly frustrating.		
Walter suffered from recurring bouts of malaria and fever.		
The death of his father and other problems led to a mental breakdown.		
He spent some time in and out of mental hospitals.		
He escaped from a mental hospital by climbing out of the window using sheets he had tied together.		
He spent his later years in a wooden shack which he kept padlocked.		
He must have been a lonely man.		
When family members entered their sanctuary, they must have been amazed.		
The colours of the paint are jewel-like.		
The creatures of the coast are displayed in their habitats.		
The sight is breathtaking.		
Few visitors to Shearwater today are allowed access to the simple shack		
a shrine to the work of this artist		
No doubt, many would love to see inside		

THE END-OF-YEAR CONCERT

Year 6 have just performed an end-of-year musical covering some of the historical events during and after the Second World War. Look at these speech bubbles and underline the **facts**.

Ten of us in the class were the evacuees. I loved it. I had to trudge round the hall among all the parents. My best friend, Haaruun, thought I looked like a complete and total misery. What was horrible was having to wear the gas mask and squeeze into the cardboard Anderson Shelter.

I enjoyed singing 'We'll Meet Again'. Seemed to set off a few tears among the audience. Maybe it was Karl's tuneless singing that did it. I played Winston Churchill. If Mum and Dad had kept quiet about having a trick cigar at home, I might have been the Queen.

I had two parts. I was in charge of the sound effects and the CD player. I did a pretty good job too. My timing was perfect. I sort of held the whole thing together in a way. I had to stand in for one of the rock 'n roll dancers when Anita was scared by Elvis's wig.

I know I'd make a great astronaut. That's probably why I was picked to play the part of Neil Armstrong. A pity the CD player jumped during the fanfare when I was planting the flag on the Moon. I just improvised a bit of moon walking. Audience loved it.

WHAT THE ACTORS THOUGHT

Those taking part in the Year 6 concert expressed some views about the show. Next to each person, write down **two** of their **opinions**.

The main idea

Strand: Comprehension

National Curriculum reference:

- identifying main ideas drawn from more than one paragraph

Reading Test / Content Domain links: 2a, 2b, 2c, 2f

THE SHANG DYNASTY

Here is some information about archaeology and the ancient Chinese civilisation known as the Shang Dynasty. Read the following paragraphs and **tick** the phrase that sums up each **main idea**.

The role of the archaeologist is to examine evidence of past civilisations. Whether they specialise in coins, weapons or pottery, they are essentially history detectives, gathering clues in order to build up a picture of how people once lived.

- past civilisations ○
- history detectives ○
- how people lived ○

It is very hard to date precisely the rise to power of the Shang Dynasty in northern China. It more or less coincided with what is referred to as the Bronze Age, when the Chinese discovered how to make bronze out of tin and copper. Many 4000-year-old bronze objects have been found.

- date of Shang Dynasty ○
- Bronze Age ○
- many objects found ○

Around this period, another remarkable development was taking place. Evidence of the invention of writing has been provided by the discovery of oracle bones. Similar to Egyptian hieroglyphics, their writing was based on pictures that represented ideas.

- discovery of oracle ○
- Egyptian hieroglyphics ○
- invention of writing ○

The king and his priests or advisers would have had important decisions to make. They would use oracle bones to predict the future or decide on a course of action. They would consult the bones on questions of military action, whether or not the king was likely to have an heir, or if it was likely to be sunny.

- kings and priests ○
- oracle bones ○
- predicting the future ○

A priest would carve the king's question on an oracle bone (often this would be a turtle bone). He then heated a bronze pin and held it against the bone, causing a series of cracks to appear on the surface of the bone. An oracle reader, usually a woman, would be called upon to interpret the pattern of cracks and provide the king with an answer.

the priest's task

the oracle reader

reading the bone

Much of what we know about the Shang Dynasty comes from the archaeological excavations of tombs. It is clear that there was a strong belief in the power of gods, but that the only way of communicating with them and seeking their favour was indirectly through the spirits of the dead. The graves of ancestors had, therefore, to be well tended with the provision of food in bronze vessels and regular ritual sacrifices.

excavation of tombs

power of gods

contacting the gods

ritual sacrifices

From the two pieces of text above, write down a **detail** that supports the following ideas:

1. The priest caused a series of cracks on the oracle bone.

___

2. The oracle reader provided the king with an answer to his question.

___

3. Archaeologists have discovered a lot about the Shang Dynasty.

___

4. The graves of ancestors had to be well tended.

___

THE SPORTING LIFE

Here are some sports commentaries from a school newsletter. **Underline** a **phrase** or a **clause** that captures the **main idea**.

The football team has had a successful season so far, which is, perhaps, the reason why Mr Chowdray feels able to make some changes, naming two new players in the line-up this afternoon. Whether this affects the shape of the team remains to be seen. But we all know how eager David and Bartek have been to win a place.

Our very own Harriet in Class 6B, the region's tennis number 3, now says she's in better shape than ever. Following last month's knee injury, her recovery has been swift. Everything will depend on her state of game fitness. There are some tough games ahead, but her trainer Mrs Jones has high hopes.

Last week, our rugby team did not impress. The younger members of the team had been given an opportunity to shine, but they unquestionably missed a great opportunity as well as several tries.

Carla says she was nervous seconds before the start of the 100m free style race for the county championship, but her butterflies soon disappeared. Once in the water, she took the lead immediately and held on to it right to the end. Somehow she can turn nerves into energy.

Netball captain, Janine, says that her gamble has paid off. Lagging behind for much of the season, her decision to spend time working on a faster, more attacking style has left opponents standing. The new approach was risky at times, but the team's higher position in the local league says it all.

PANTOMIME

The following paragraphs about pantomime are made up of a **main idea** plus supporting **details.** Identify the **main idea**.

Every Christmas, local theatres put on stage a traditional pantomime. Whatever the subject-matter, there is a familiarity to them each year. You can expect songs, dancing (especially by the two people who are inside the silly horse or cow outfit), slapstick comedy, a lot of humour and a storyline based very loosely on a fairytale, with plenty of extra, topical material.

The main idea is:

Everyone at some time must have called out: 'It's behind you!' or 'Yes, it is!' The audience expects the pantomime experience to be one of participation. Booing at the wicked step-mother or the man with the black moustache, who has just entered stage left, is all part of the fun.

The main idea is:

In the Middle Ages, the Mummers Play was a regular, folk performance in villages up and down the country. But the pantomime as we know it today has a number of different influences, mainly from Europe. In Italy, the commedia dell'arte was a popular form of travelling theatre. There and later in France, professional clowns improvised comic stories that often contained moral lessons for the gathered crowds. Each story had the same recognisable characters and usually contained a very messy chase scene.

The main idea is:

BEES

Here is some information about bees. Each paragraph is made up of three sentences: the **main idea** and two supporting details. Underline the **main idea.**

Bees may be appear to be quite insignificant but they are an essential part of our lives. Along with other insects, they pollinate most of our fruit and vegetables. Without them, the world's farming and our supply of food would suffer.

When you think of bees, you probably think of honey. But bees provide us with much more. The marmalade on your breakfast toast, the fruit juice and apple you had earlier, and the tomatoes on your pizza were all brought to you courtesy of bees.

The bee you are most likely to see is the honey bee, though there are 260 different types in the UK. These can be classified as either social bees or solitary bees. Solitary bees tend to be smaller than honey bees and bumblebees, and live in pairs rather than with a queen, drones and workers.

Many wild bumblebees and solitary bees are disappearing at an alarming rate. Little wonder, therefore, that researchers are trying to understand what is causing their decline. There are a number of threats: habitat loss, pesticides, disease and climate change.

Some ornamental garden flowers may look fantastic but many have been bred in such a way to contain no nectar. This, of course, doesn't apply to all garden plants. You can help bees to survive and increase in number by observing which flowers they like and planting those.

As busy as a bee, a hive of activity, making a beeline, the bees knees – these are just a few of common phrases in our language. Such idioms alone testify to the central role bees play in our lives. And did you know that Dumbledore is also a Cornish word for bumblebee?

Summarising main ideas

Strand: Comprehension

National Curriculum reference:

- identifying main ideas drawn from more than one paragraph and summarising these

Reading Test / Content Domain links: 2a, 2b, 2c, 2f

SUBHEADINGS

Write **subheadings** for these short texts. A good subheading should immediately tell the reader what the text is about. This is very helpful when a reader is scanning any piece of non-fiction or a web page looking for answers to questions.

____

Home-made ice cream contains cream, sugar and fruit. The cream can be infused with vanilla flavouring. Fruit, such as raspberries or blackcurrants, are puréed before being mixed in. The result is then churned and frozen.

____

The sandwich is named after the 4th Earl of Sandwich, an 18th century aristocrat, who ordered his servant to bring him meat tucked between two pieces of bread, so that he could eat and play cards at the same time.

____

Using your fridge properly helps to prevent food poisoning. Raw meat and fish should be covered and stored on the bottom shelf of the fridge. Any leftover food should first be placed in a sealed container. Salad and vegetables should be stored in the drawers which are usually at the bottom of the fridge.

____

Hands have the potential for spreading germs. Always wash hands thoroughly with warm, soapy water. Rinse and dry properly before starting to prepare food as well as after you've finished. It is especially important to wash your hands after handling raw meat and before touching ready-to-eat food.

____

The Summer Challenge this year at school was better than ever. Thirteen contestants from Year 6 plus our brave Deputy Head stepped up to the mark in our Worst Cake Baker Contest. There were two rules: cakes must contain no poisonous ingredients or anything still living. Needless to say, Maxine in class 6B won with her Oozing Gastropod Delight. The other contestants will now have to have a plateful each.

____

Cooking is a great way to sharpen life-skills (as well as your set of kitchen knives!) From how to make meringues to how to eat them politely without infuriating the rest of the family with your hideous eating habits, preparing and serving food is part of learning all about life. Acceptance on one of our cookery courses will open the kitchen door to fresh opportunities. So ditch that old, stale life now and join us.

LOSING THE PLOT

When following the plot of fantasy stories, you have to pay close attention. Read this story line from a computer game and then number the events in the correct order.

Aryth arrives at Castle Hazard with Crow perched, as always, on his shoulder. He overhears a conversation between Prince Ynyr and the half-reptilian sorceress, Malsaura, planning a conspiracy to overthrow Princess Ameira – a successful ruler – with the aid of her all-seeing amulet. He travels to the Cave-dwellers to ask if they will make him a sword capable of killing the sorceress. He has almost completed his week-long journey through the Dunes of the Scorpions when he is attacked by the Gargantua, a giant tribe of snake worshippers, who throw him into a deep pit to be disposed of by King Kobrah. Doors in the walls of the pit open to reveal not one but seven other Kobrahs. On all sides, fangs approach Aryth. But a screech heralds the arrival of Crow, who flies down and pecks out the eyes of King Kobrah. This causes a fighting frenzy among the other snakes, all eager to become pack leader. Quickly, Aryth escapes with Crow through one of the doors into a labyrinth that leads through the magma lakes to the Cave-dwellers who make him a sword. Unfortunately, he is met at the mouth of the cave by Prince Ynyr and Malsaura. However, the ever-watchful Princess Ameira has sent her soldiers to protect Aryth. The Prince is captured but Malsaura disappears.

- [ ] **The sorceress appears at the mouth of the cave**
- [ ] **Crow comes to Aryth's rescue**
- [ ] **Aryth overhears a conspiracy**
- [ ] **The cave-dwellers make Aryth a sword**
- [ ] **Aryth and Crow cross the Dunes of the Scorpions**
- [ ] **Aryth escapes through a labyrinth**
- [ ] **The Gargantua capture Aryth**

WHAT'S THE POINT?

These short pieces of text are all constructed around a **main idea** that isn't necessarily contained in any particular single sentence. Alongside each text, write a short sentence summing up what it is about.

Green plants draw up water and other nutrients from the soil by means of their roots. They take in carbon dioxide through their leaves. But without the light from the sun the leaves wouldn't be able to use these resources to produce food.

____

____

____

Habitat is the location of a food chain of plants and animals: consumers, prey and predators. In the cycle of life and death, animal waste and animal and plant remains provide the nutrients that plants need to produce healthy growth.

____

____

____

Animal species have evolved in an abundance of different ways. Without such adaptations to particular environments, they could not exist. Some examples are the beaks and talons of hawks, the camouflage of zebras and the gills of fish.

____

____

____

ANTI-BULLYING ASSEMBLY

Here is a rough layout of a poster that some children have been working on in preparation for a class assembly. They have numbered certain parts of it that still need working on.

1

2
Bullying can happen anywhere and to anyone – at work, in the street, at school. It can also take place on the internet on social media like Facebook, Snapchat, etc.

3
Being bullied, because it is something that is experienced repeatedly, can lead to depression, lack of confidence, fear, anxiety, loneliness and poor school work.

4
teasing – name-calling – spreading rumours and lies – leaving someone out on purpose – being rude about your family, your clothes or where you live

5
threatening to hurt you – hitting – stealing your property – breaking your things – spitting – pulling hair – biting

6
report the cyberbully – block the cyberbully – take a screenshot of the bullying – talk to an adult that you trust

7 PLAYGROUND
remember it's not your fault – talk to a teacher or parent – contact ChildLine on 0800 1111

1. The children need a title for their poster. What might it be?

2. A sub-heading is needed for the section numbered 2. What do you suggest?

3. A common feature of bullying is mentioned in section 3. What is it?

4. What sub-heading would you give section 3?

5. Sections 4 and 5 both list the different forms that bullying can take. What is the difference between the two lists?

6. Make up a sub-heading for section 6.

7. The sub-heading for section 7 doesn't say enough about the content of that section. Can you improve it?

8. If you had to introduce the topic of the assembly in a sentence or two, what would you say?

Details that support the main idea

Strand: Comprehension

National Curriculum reference:

- identifying main ideas drawn from more than one paragraph and summarising these

Reading Test / Content Domain links: 2a, 2b, 2c, 2f

AN EYE FOR DETAIL

Here is a list of **main ideas** in the form of thought bubbles. The right-hand column presents a list of **details**. Draw lines matching up each **main idea** with the appropriate **detail.**

Sanjay has been saving his pocket money for a new bicycle.

I don't know anybody who is crazier about animals than Kira.

I think I could make extra money as a dog-walker.

A good mountain bike, if it's well cared for, should last years.

Shopkeepers don't like you taking your dog in the shop.

I fell off my bike when a dog ran in front of me.

Lots of people in our road don't have time to walk their dogs.

Kira always has to tie her Labrador outside the bakery.

You don't see him spending so much in the shopping mall.

Whoever was looking after the dog wasn't doing a good job.

Her favourite has got to be her Labrador, Blackie.

There's no point saving for something then neglecting it.

SCIENTIFIC IDEAS

Here are some **main ideas** from your science lessons. Find the **detail** that goes with each of them. One has already been done for you.

- We use materials according to their properties.
- Electrical components will function in different ways depending on power source.
- Photosynthesis in plants requires water, light from the sun and carbon dioxide.
- Forces include gravity, air resistance, upthrust and magnetism.
- Rocks are formed in a number of different ways.
- Some processes are not reversible.
- Food chains are composed of producers and consumers.
- The factors not being studied in a fair test must be kept constant.
- Some substances will dissolve in water.
- The Moon is a satellite that orbits the Earth.

- Melting chocolate can change its state back to a solid.
- By producing their own food, plants are fundamental to life on the planet.
- In scientific experiments, it is essential to change one variable at a time.
- A bulb won't light up if its circuit is not complete or it doesn't have a battery.
- Some light passes through translucent materials.
- The movement of objects in space depends on gravity.
- Examples of soluble materials include salt and sugar.
- The transportation of water throughout a plant begins with the roots.
- Igneous rock such as basalt is created inside volcanoes.
- Friction is the force involved when a cyclist brakes.

SUMMER FESTIVAL

Here are some headlines describing a summer music festival. From the three possibilities, tick **one detail** that supports the **main idea** contained in the headline.

Heavens Open But No Sign Of Dampened Spirits

The cows in the adjacent field took shelter. ______

It was very late by the time the last members of the audience arrived. ______

The mood at the festival was terrific as usual. ______

Record Numbers Of Fans Fill The Fields

Fans brought their own music to share with new friends. ______

Some late-comers found it hard to find somewhere to pitch a tent. ______

It was so hot the sale of fans broke an all-time record. ______

Headline Band A Well-Kept Secret

The drummer has left after a dispute with his manager. ______

Rumours suggest that the organisers are having problems. ______

Our reporter has some inside information on possible highlights. ______

Satellites Send Saturday Songs To The World

Organisers plan to extend the audience next year. ______

The top band and other highlights plan a world tour. ______

This new live link-up has people dancing from Chile to China. ______

YOUR DAILY CARBS

Here is an information leaflet about healthy eating. What is it mainly about?

Carbohydrates

As far as health is concerned, the type of carbohydrate you eat is possibly more important than the amount. There are two basic types: simple sugars and complex starch. This is important since all the carbohydrates we consume are turned into glucose and carried by the bloodstream to our cells and organs.

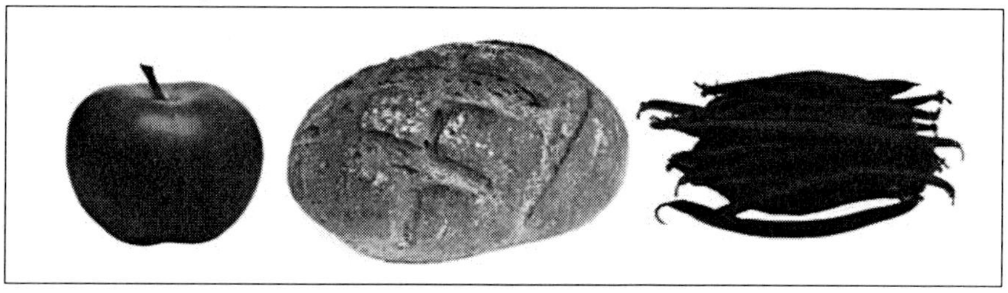

The healthiest sources of carbohydrate include wholemeal bread, pasta, rice, fruit, vegetables and beans. Less healthy examples are those that have been refined during the factory process, such as white sugar, white bread, cakes, fizzy drinks and sweets.

What is the leaflet mainly about? Tick the correct one.

Healthiest sources of carbohydrate ◯

The body turns carbohydrates into glucose ◯

There are two types of carbohydrate ◯

Write a sentence from the leaflet that helped you to make your choice:

____

____

Inferences

Strand: Making inferences

National Curriculum reference:

- drawing inferences such as inferring characters' feelings, thoughts and motives from their actions

Reading Test / Content Domain links: 2a, 2b, 2d, 2f, 2g

RIDDLES

Try to work out the answers to these riddles from the clues provided.

I'm a single candle on a cake,
A solar trip without a break,
Cheer me out and hear me ringing,
Fifty-two weeks and a new beginning.

I have a head and I have a tail -
Of that I am quite certain.
See me cast inside a pig or sail
Through air into a fountain.

The rich, they need this.
The poor have plenty.
If you only eat this,
Your belly will be empty.

If I have it, I don't share it.
If I share it, I don't have it.
If the world knows, then it doesn't exist.

Looking through walls
Was the maker's intention.
That's why he came up
With this common invention.

I lose my head in the morning light,
But get it back in the dark of night.

SAYING ONE THING AND FEELING ANOTHER

People don't always say exactly how they are feeling, but often you can still tell. Draw lines matching the speech to the correct emotion.

"Of course, it's a free country. If the neighbours feel it's ok to play loud music all hours of the night, well, I suppose that's their business."	**overwhelmed**
"Yes, he is my dad. No, I don't know why he likes wearing that Christmas sweater in August. He says it shows off his dance moves."	**optimistic**
"We are ahead in the league, and, we have recently bought a number of top-ranking players but I always say we take one game at a time."	**ambitious**
"Hello, could you possibly send the fire brigade. Where am I? Dangling from the window ledge. What's that? Hang on? Yes all right."	**annoyed**
"Some say that my musical will take London by storm, that no one has ever attempted to put six top bands on stage. But, hey, that's just me."	**downhearted**
"Juggling three jobs, looking after four children, elderly parents, a houseful of cats and a parrot that's stopped talking to me! I'm fine!"	**desperate**
"Could have been worse. Lowest marks in the entire school. Dad says I could have got the lowest marks in the entire country... I suppose."	**embarrassed**

SHERLOCK'S NOT HOME

Detectives have to be careful when looking for clues at the scene of a crime. Why do you think the detective did the following things?

1. He wore gloves before entering the house.

   ____

2. He checked behind the door before entering.

   ____

3. He opened the fridge and sniffed the open carton of milk.

   ____

   ____

4. He put his hand close to the side of the kettle.

   ____

   ____

5. He picked up a cup by pushing a pencil through its handle.

   ____

   ____

6. He looked in every room to see if all the mirrors and pictures were straight.

   ____

   ____

7. He opened the window and looked outside.

   ____

   ____

A PENNY FOR YOUR THOUGHTS

Words and body language tell us how someone is feeling or what they are thinking. Sometimes, however, the way something is said will give more accurate information, whereas words can be used to hide thoughts and feelings. Fill in the thought bubbles to show what each character is really feeling inside.

Yes, I did let in that last-minute goal in the hockey match, but... you know... win some, lose some.

Jerry's always making fun of my accent. It doesn't bother me. That's just the way he is – a bit of a joker.

I'm glad you liked my dad and his talk about hairstyles of the 50s. You're right. He did look great in the different wigs.

Oh, yeah, I'm looking forward to the exam tomorrow. I'm sure I've done enough work, so I should be fine.

This is a picture of me beside a bush. Here I am standing in a bush. Here, I'm quite close to a bush. Fantastic holiday.

Spiders. They are fascinating creatures. I can't think why anybody would be scared of them. So many legs.

MEDIEVAL FANTASY

Here is part of a fantasy story. The questions that follow require you to use your **inferential** skills – your ability to read between the lines.

Faylinn's Revenge

"You ready, Baalfire? We're waitin'. Get your twinkletoes in some boots and get out here!" Even my friend, Tom, with his failing hearing, couldn't mistake the rasping voice of Harald Ruffsnape, as coarse as bracken across the skin. He thumps the door in time to my name: "Vin – cent – Baal – fire!" The goats bleat in their stall; the mice scramble in the thatch of the roof.

Opening the door, I push his hand away as he reaches out to prod me, as usual, in the shoulder. He grins. "When you goin' to tie a pretty ribbon in that hair of yours and be a proper girl?" I save my reply for another day.

The evening's entertainment is to follow the ancient creature known as Faylinn, a well-known figure. A harmless hermit who huddles in a stinking cave on the other side of the river, she is taunted by the local children: imitating her hobble, throwing stones, daring each other. We pray that our dreams will contain no sight or sound of that creepy, old witch. But every night we wake up bawling like kittens in a sack.

The sun has gone but a glimmering cut of light shows Faylinn dragging a branch behind her. Kindling for her fire, I reckon. Her face is smoke black. We follow, but soon the fingers of darkness begin to close around us. Stunted trees are grey ghosts crouching among the swirls of marsh gas as she disappears into her cave. It's a poisonous place. The air catches throats.

"That's a filthy hole," says Tom, giggling. "It's filthier than the biggest pile of filth I've ever seen." This earns him a familiar slap that knocks him to the ground. The others laugh awkwardly. No one is prepared to help him up except me. I narrow my eyes. Harald glares back. The others wait. The moment passes.

"See that smoke whifflin' out of the cracks in them rocks. That's Faylinn talking with imps and demons of all varieties. So all you pipsqueakin' chickens, get ready with your howlin' and hollerin'."

A heartbeat barely passes when a burning ember comes spitting out of the cave mouth, making an arc through the sour air. Then another and another. Here and there, the marsh gas bursts into flames. The treetops come alive and black shadows swoop about our heads, disturbed even more by our screaming terror. We scramble in all directions, till we all turn to find ourselves face to face with Faylinn. The evil grin. Three front teeth like chiselled stalactites. She points and growls something under her breath. "Good evening, sprouts," is all she says, but what we hear is a curse.

We run for it chased by nothing more than our own moon shadows. But no one turns to check. Least of all Harald. Somehow, those fat knees of his carry his wheezing body a good fifty yards in front of everybody else. Now that did us all a power of good.

1. What sort of person is Harald Ruffsnape? Write down a piece of evidence to support your answer.

____

____

2. Who is telling the story?

____

3. What clues are there to suggest the story is set in medieval times?

____

____

4. What evidence is there to suggest that Vincent is not frightened of Harald?

____

____

5. Why do you think Faylinn is taunted by the local children?

____

6. What would cause her face to be described as 'smoke black'?

____

7. What are the 'grey ghosts crouching among the swirls of the marsh gas'?

____

8. Why do you think Tom giggles when he talks about the cave?

____

____

9. Who slaps Tom?

____

10. Why do you think 'the others laugh awkwardly'?

____

____

11. 'The others wait.' What are they waiting for?

____

____

12. How does the burning ember come out of the cave?

____

13. What are the black shadows that swoop about their heads?

____

14. What makes them think they've been cursed?

____

____

15. What does the second last sentence tell us about Harald?

____

16. 'Now that did us all a power of good.' This final remark suggests that things might be a bit different in the future. In what way?

____

____

Justifying inferences with evidence

Strand: Making inferences

National Curriculum reference:

- drawing inferences such as inferring characters' feelings, thoughts and motives from their actions, and justifying inferences with evidence

Reading Test / Content Domain links: 2a, 2b, 2d, 2f, 2g

BETWEEN THE LINES

Use your inferential skills to look for clues about what is happening in these scenes.

> Rajeev kicked his neighbour's fence. He smacked the top of his head. He could see Mrs Collins staring from her kitchen window with that look on her face. She glanced at the broken heads of her daffodils and Reg, her Alsatian, a chain attached to its collar, sitting a few feet away from the football in the middle of her perfect lawn.
>
> "So what are you waiting for?" said Meena, Rajeev's sister.
>
> "Yeah," said his friend, Tom. "You can climb the fence. Look! Reg isn't going anywhere."
>
> Rajeev sighed and directed Tom's gaze to the other end of the dog's chain.

1. What has happened?

____

2. How do you know?

____

____

3. Do you think that this is something that has happened before?

____

4. What makes you think that?

____

____

5. How do you know Mrs Collins is a keen gardener?

____

6. How do you know Meena and Tom don't think it is their problem?

____

____

7. Why does Rajeev point to the other end of the dog's chain?

____

Jason slammed the door behind him, dropped his jacket and kicked it into the corner, threw his homework across the living-room floor and headed for the fridge. As his mother would be home late from office, he spent the evening on the sofa with his feet on a tower of homework books, a slowly diminishing pizza balanced on his stomach and the TV remote in his hand. His mother found him there fast asleep at 10:30pm.

The following day meant another late shift for his mother. So, when he let himself in, the first thing he did was retrieve the pizza box from the day before, fold his school report inside it, and shove to the bottom of the bin in the shed. Then he went to the kitchen in order to cook his mother's favourite supper.

1. How is Jason feeling when he returns home from school?

____

2. How do you know how he is feeling?

____

____

3. Do you think Jason's school report is good one?

____

4. Why do you think this?

____

____

5. How do you think Jason's report turned out the way it did?

____

____

6. Why does Jason prepare his mother's favourite supper?

____

____

Jess stood in the doorway of their country cottage, not quite outside in the sharp air where, a week ago, there would have been sound of cattle waiting to be milked; nor inside beside the familiar warmth of the stove. Mum and Dad and her brother, Ben, loaded the van. Ben glared at her as he pushed past her for another chest full of books. She caught his disapproval, but she didn't care. Her friends at school had all said that London would be an adventure and they promised to try to organise a get-together. She sighed, unable to move. It was almost as if she were paralysed.

1. What time of year do you think it is?

___

2. Why do you think this?

___

3. What sort of work have her parents been involved in up to now?

___

4. What evidence is there to support your answer?

___

5. What is happening?

___

6. How do you know?

___

7. What is Ben thinking?

___

8. How does Jess feel about what is going on?

___

9. Jess doesn't expect to see her friends again. How do you know?

___

QUEEN OF THE AIR

Amelia Earhart: first woman to fly solo across the Atlantic.

Born – 24 July 1897

Disappeared – 2 July 1937

Amelia Earhart, an American, experienced her first close encounter with an aeroplane at the Iowa State Fair. She was ten years old and described it as: '... a thing of rusty wire and wood and not at all interesting.'

Almost ten years later, while at a stunt-flying exhibition, an airborne pilot spotted Amelia and a friend, standing away from the rest of the crowd. He swooped down towards them, possibly hoping to make them run, but Amelia stood her ground. Later in life, she said: 'I did not understand it at the time, but I believe that little red airplane [aeroplane] said something to me as it swished by.'

On 28 December 1920, pilot Frank Hawks took her up in an aeroplane for the first time. 'By the time I had got two or three hundred feet off the ground, I knew I had to fly.'

As a child, Amelia stayed with her grandmother during school term. In spite of her grandmother's disapproval – common in those days – Amelia spent much of her time outdoors, climbing trees, riding imaginary horses and hunting. Later, in high school, she was described as:

A.E. – the girl in brown who walks alone.

On 3 January 1921, she took her first flying lesson. She worked hard for six months and saved enough money to buy her first, small aircraft: a two-seater biplane painted bright yellow, which she called *The Canary*.

A few years later, she was invited to join two other pilots to fly across the Atlantic. They left Newfoundland and landed in Wales 21 hours later. She became an international celebrity.

Then a new secret project presented itself – the opportunity to fly the same route completely single-handed. The news soon got out and on 20 May, 1932, she took off for Paris, but icy conditions and strong winds forced her to land in a farmer's field in Londonderry, Ireland. At a time when even a car was a novelty, one can only imagine how excited the local people must have felt to see her land her plane.

Approaching her 40th birthday, she decided to be the first woman to fly round the world. By 29 June 1937, with her navigator, Fred Noonan, she reached New Guinea, having completed 22,000 of the 29,000 mile journey. A few days later, running into cloud and heavy rain, and with broken and irregular radio guidance from a ship in the area, her last message was: 'We must be on you, but we cannot see you. Fuel is running low. Been unable to reach you by radio. We are flying at 1,000 feet. We are running north and south.' Nothing more was heard from her.

Now use evidence from the text to answer the following questions.

1. What, in the introduction to the text, suggests that we don't know precisely when Amelia Earhart died.

2. Amelia wasn't impressed when she first had a close-up view of an aeroplane. How do we know?

3. What experience, described by Amelia, tells you that, even as a child, she was brave and not easily scared?

4. Why might her grandmother have disapproved of Amelia spending so much of her time outdoors?

5. How do we know Amelia had trouble making friends at school?

6. What phrase tells you that her second Atlantic crossing was done on her own?

7. Why would the local people in Ireland be so excited about Amelia landing there?

8. What made flying so difficult on the last leg of the round-the-world flight?

Predicting what might happen

Strand: Making inferences

National Curriculum reference:

- predicting what might happen from details stated and implied

Reading Test / Content Domain links: 2a, 2b, 2g

THEN WHAT DID THEY SAY?

Using the hints given in these pieces of conversation, write down what you think might have been said in response.

1. "Megan! Alesha is standing here, waiting with her hula hoop. What shall I tell her?"

____

2. "Excuse me, young man. Can you help? I want some biscuits from that top shelf."

____

____

3. "I think we've seen this film before, Simon, but I can't remember how it ends."

____

4. "Hi, Emilia. Just back from holidays? What was the best thing you did?"

____

5. "So how are you going to explain why you didn't finish your homework?"

____

6. "What happened when the referee blew his whistle?"

____

7. "I would have been scared by that growling too. So what did you do?"

____

8. "Once you reached the top of the tower, what could you see?"

____

9. "Why do you think you didn't get picked for the team?"

____

FUTURIST MOVIES

Here are some scenes from films. Put yourself in the place of the characters in order to explain where they were, what happened next or what was said.

Chen kicked the rusty casing of an abandoned torch – some 21st century thing – down the slope. It toppled and rolled over the disintegrating carpet, clattering against broken seats, until it came to rest against a raised platform. It could have been a stage. It was hard to tell. A mouldering curtain covered most of it. "What is this place? What happened here?"

Chen almost jumped out of his skin when a shadowy figure behind him said:

"

____

____

____"

They spent some days crossing the footsore desert. Lou started grumbling about turning back after the first hour, but she trudged along behind her grandmother. They took turns pulling the sled piled high with their belongings. On the fifth day, they had to bind their faces with rags against the sand-blasting wind. Beneath the wind's howls, Lou thought she could make out the toll of a bell. "Keep going, Lou," said Grandma. "Almost there."

Then, as quickly as it had been summoned up, the wind dropped. There, on the horizon, was an immense spike rupturing the surface. It could have been the nose-cone of a rocket ship. But as they got closer, Lou realised it was the source of the earlier ringing sound.

Grandma sighed, took a gulp of water from her flask and said:

"

____

____

____"

Joni and Kazuo cautiously emerged from the shelter of their cave. For a month, they had restricted themselves to what meagre food supplies they had managed to carry, as well as the occasional roasted lizard – a special treat.

The meteorite shower, at first a spectacular night-time display, had steadily bombarded a vast area, the tremors vibrating their ribcages even in the depths of their protective mountain.

As they walked towards the brow of the hill overlooking the city, Joni took Kazuo's hand. On top of the ridge, they looked down and saw...

♎♐♑♒●⌘☒❖♌■❍

From her cage, day after day, Morgana the chimpanzee watched with quiet curiosity the work of the surrounding scientists. Reluctantly, they had concluded that no amount of intelligence-enhancing exercises, games or videos could increase her natural, mental abilities. And in the evening, her keeper, Frank Green, had pushed paper and crayons and kids' toys through the bars along with her supper, in the hope that he might succeed where the scientists had failed.

What none of the scientific team expected was to return in the morning to find the cage empty and a note, scrawled in coloured crayons, that said:

WHAT DO I DO NOW?

21st Century, rock-guitar playing teenager, Vinny, has been left alone in the family mansion. His father, Sir Peter Balfour, an eccentric scientist, is giving a talk in New York about his experiments on the brains of reptiles and human beings.

Use the information available to decide what Vinny does next.

Outrageously loud, heavy metal crescendo, a decibel louder than the wind outside. Just my mobile under a stack of pizza boxes. Dad has sent a video message. Can I really be bothered opening it? He's more interested in being on a screen than talking to me.

"Vinny..." he begins. He's whispering and glancing over his shoulder. And that's it. That's all there is and the thing goes blank. Then the heavy front doors crash open.

As I'm checking all the other locks, there's an enormous thump on the back door. Not an out-of-hours visitor, or the wild wind. No, this is like the shoulder of a rhino, a bunch of guys ramming it with a log, a demolition ball. Somebody wants to get inside. Desperately. I'm thinking of the video cut short and the experiments Dad does in his private upstairs lab. There's a secret in this house and it's like the people who want it... want it now. If only the video told me a bit more. Maybe there's another message.

The past awaits at the next turn

I'm thinking about all the rules that have surrounded my life. About not doing this, not going there. Some questions unanswered. Rooms of the house that are locked and stay locked. A sudden guttural howling outside. I need to do something apart from running back and forward like some wind-up toy doing a traditional stupidity dance. Then another crash somewhere in the house. Somebody has broken in.

There's a familiar cry upstairs. 'Well, Vinny Balfour," I mutter to myself, "you may be a thirteen-year-old, slightly weird, withdrawn, good-for-nothing, spoiled brat with poor SATs results, who needs a haircut, a thorough wash and probably a good talking to, and who mutters to himself, but you'd never leave without Kitty." Got to find her and get out of here fast. It's a big place, this house, with stairs to match. Her cries lead me to a door I've never opened before. And inside, it's strange. I'm surrounded by rolled-up, cobwebbed maps, an out-of-date globe, bottles of stuff, a bundle of stinking clothes in one corner and piles of mouldering books.

The moonlight breaches the room's one stained-glass window in an oily rainbow of colours. They splash across the wall, throwing light along a wall of paintings of reptilian creatures with human faces. In the middle of the room, Kitty is standing on a wooden chest and snarling like an angry dog. Footsteps on the stairs are closing. What now?

Features of texts

Strand: Comprehension / Themes and Conventions

National Curriculum reference:

- identifying how language, structure and presentation contribute to meaning
- identifying themes and conventions in a wide range of books

Reading Test / Content Domain links: 2a, 2b, 2f, 2g

RAINBOWS

Each one of these texts is about the same thing: rainbows. They are, however, written in different styles. Check how their features differ and decide whether they are from a diary, a letter, a science book, a poem or a newspaper article.

Last night, 11 year-old Georgina Stafford, of Priory Lane, Norton, sent in this wonderful photograph of the double rainbow that graced the skies yesterday afternoon over Sutton Hill. Georgina said, "I was out walking Rinty when I looked up and there it was."

____

Spent the day wading through my spelling list. I've been feeling very nervous about tomorrow's exam. Dad says the cat can spell better than me. Thanks, Dad!!! I was feeling pretty miserable. It was pouring. Then I saw the rainbow. Maybe it's a sign. Hope so.

____

Sunlight, though white in appearance, consists of a spectrum of different colours. During rain, as light rays from the sun enter each water droplet and are reflected back to your eye at an angle of approximately 40°, the rays are separated into a familiar spectrum. To view a rainbow, you must be facing the direction of the rainfall with your back to the sun.

____

Random flags invading the corn
Oh for a rhyme for impossible fruit
Yearning for sunlight the moment we're born
Grass after rainfall – scent underfoot
Billowing sky shakes off its frown
Ink of the evening after sundown
Visiting bees circle around.

____

I would like to point out that this is not the first time I have raised this issue. Some light at the end of the tunnel (or, to use another metaphor: a rainbow after the storm) would be a reply stating that the council has a plan to deal with seagulls.

____

<u>TEXT DETECTIVE</u>

The following texts have been put under the magnifying glass, so that only a part of them is showing. From the evidence available, decide whether they are from:

- a review in a magazine
- an instruction manual
- a 'for sale' ad
- a biography
- a reference book
- a novel

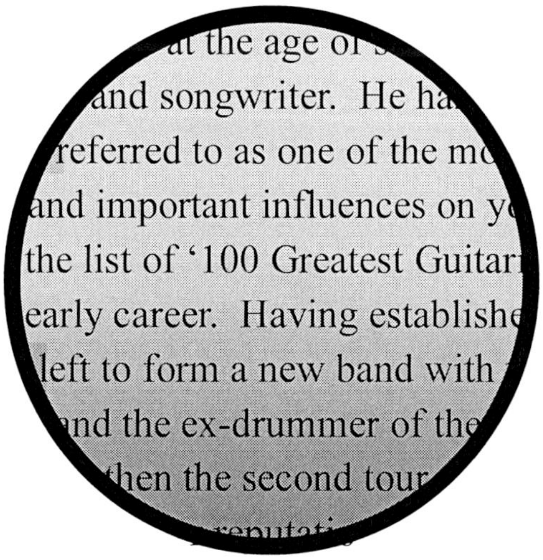

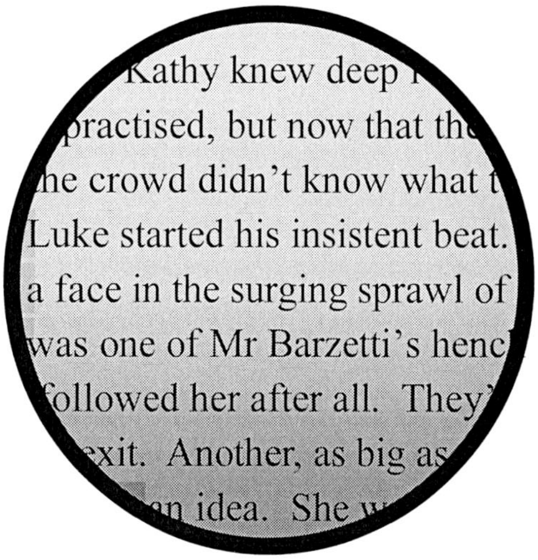

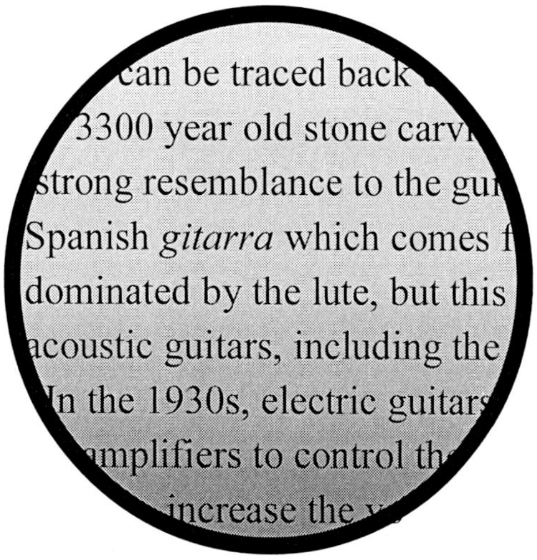

The final piece of text is not in the list:

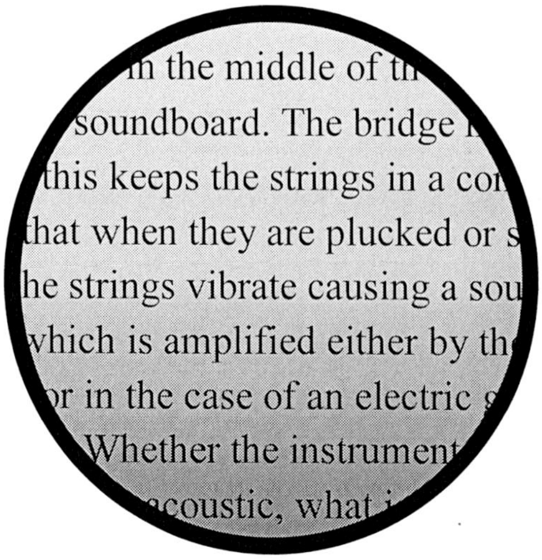

ARGUMENT

We often think of people 'having an argument' as the same as 'having a row'. An argument is also where a particular point of view is presented in a clear and convincing way.

Should Fizzy Drinks Be Banned?

The consumption of fizzy drinks is identified as an important health issue in the UK. Recent research confirms that there is a link between drinking too much sugar- and caffeine-based products and tooth decay and obesity, and more serious conditions such as diabetes. Inevitably, this is the cause of deterioration in the health of individuals, but also increased pressure on the National Health Service.

Ask any school-age child or teenager why they like fizzy drinks and they will no doubt tell you that they are delicious, refreshing and very convenient. They are readily available from supermarkets, fast-food outlets and vending machines. Great when you're thirsty and in a hurry. They also give you an immediate buzz.

It could be argued, however, that this is the result of successful advertising and marketing campaigns on the part of the drinks manufacturers. On the one hand, fizzy drinks are presented as a cool way to quench your thirst, while, on the other, their calorie content causes dehydration.

The facts of the case are that these drinks have no nutritional value whatsoever. Sugar-laden (and many sugar-free) drinks unquestionably lead to overweight and associated heart problems, and to diabetes and related damage to the body.

Those in favour of sweetened, carbonated drinks would maintain that there is no harm done, that it's just a bit of fun, and that we should not be restricting the individual's freedom to choose what they eat and drink. This, admittedly, is very persuasive. With this in mind, in a world that is increasingly health-conscious, perhaps we need to take a more persuasive approach.

An educational programme may be required. One that overturns the teenage idea that they need the caffeine (an addictive ingredient) in 'energy drinks' and convinces younger children that many of the so-called 'fruit drinks' contain no fruit at all. The hope would be that, with accurate, science-based information, people would be in a position to make more informed and healthy decisions.

1. How do you know what the argument is about?

____

2. Give an example of the **passive voice** being used.

____

3. What verb tense is used? Give an example.

____

____

4. Find examples of **three** descriptive words that defenders of fizzy drinks are like to use.

____

5. Write down an example of a connecting phrase that you are likely to find in any balanced argument.

____

6. Find **two** scientific facts that are given in favour of banning fizzy drinks.

____

____

7. What persuasive argument is put forward against such a ban?

____

8. Find **two** examples of technical words or phrases used in the argument.

____

9. In the conclusion, the writer appears to have changed their argument slightly. What is their conclusion?

____

____

Features of texts and meaning

Strand: Comprehension / Themes and Conventions

National Curriculum reference:

- identifying how language, structure and presentation contribute to meaning
- recognising some different forms of poetry
- identifying themes and conventions in a wide range of books

Reading Test / Content Domain links: 2a, 2b, 2f, 2g

THE SCHOOL LETTER

A letter has been sent home about a special day for Year 6. Look at the content and features of the letter and answer the questions.

Green Wood School

Headteacher: A. Dalrymple BA, PhD
Head of Governors: R. Whittaker

6 October 2015

Dear Parents / Carers,

All day on Monday 9th November, Year 6 will be participating in an exciting Indian Experience. This is being organised by Mrs Clitheroe to launch our new, international link with Mandir Central School in Rajasthan. Both Year 6 classes will have an opportunity to try out some of the moves of classical Indian dance styles, as well as more contemporary Bollywood style dances – all of which will be demonstrated by children in our link school via Skype. This is scheduled for the morning as there is a 4 ½ hour time difference between schools.

Lunch will consist of tasting a range of vegetarian Indian foods, provided by Mr and Mrs Singh of the Taj Mahal Restaurant in the High Street.

The afternoon will be spent exploring some of the art forms, such as Rangoli floor patterns, that we associate with India – examples of which we received a few weeks ago and featured in last month's newsletter. (These can still be viewed on the school website.)

In order to cover the cost of the Indian food provided, we would be grateful if you could contribute £2.50 per child. Any parents wishing to join us for this special lunch may do so at an additional cost of £2.50 per person.

If your child has any food allergies we should be aware of, please state them on the attached form.

Finally, any adult with a current CRB (now referred to as DBS) certificate, who would like to volunteer to lend support on the day, should contact the school secretary, Mrs Williams.

Many thanks.

Yours sincerely,

A. Dalrymple

Anne Dalrymple

1. Why is this obviously a letter from school? Write down three of its features.

2. How has the headteacher immediately made it clear what the letter is about?

3. The first paragraph explains how this special day has come about. In your own words, describe the main reason behind it.

4. The first three paragraphs are ordered in a particular way to describe the day. How have they been ordered?

5. The school makes use of digital technology. Write down two examples of this.

6. The letter ends with three pieces of practical information. What are they?

DRIVERLESS CARS

Rihana and Rick in Year 6 are having a debate about driverless cars. Their teacher is looking for evidence of their skill in presenting a balanced argument.

I am going to argue that driverless cars will be the highpoint of humanity's inventiveness, and will be seen by future historians as *the* technological marvel of the digital age.

FOR

My point of view is that technology, wonderful as it is, can only go so far, and that human beings have to take responsibility for their own actions. You could say: "I've seen the movie; it was science fiction; and the robots took over."

RICK

I take your point, but look at it this way. Human beings make terrible drivers: they chat on the phone, light cigarettes, have rows with their kids in the back, drink too much beer, have heart attacks, veer left or right unexpectedly to avoid cute baby rabbits...

AGAINST

RIHANA

Exactly! What about baby rabbits? A self-drive car, fitted with cameras and sensors and satellite navigation systems has no feelings. It won't cope with the unexpected, change its mind, or be considerate to an old person thinking about crossing the road. How will it deal with temporary traffic lights or overnight floods?

Every year in the UK, 2000 people die in road accidents and 80,000 are seriously injured. They would be safer; they'd park themselves and all the passengers could read or play computer games for the whole journey. You could even go to sleep.

These are important points. I know all sorts of tests can be done on some desolate track far away from real people and the kind of everyday hazards that drivers face, but that's not enough. However, if it can be proved, under normal conditions, that they'll be safer, then ... we'll see.

1. What phrases do the two children use to make it clear that they are expressing personal opinions?

____

____

2. Rick uses **two** persuasive phrases to describe driverless cars. What are they?

____

____

3. What is Rihana's attitude to new technology?

____

____

4. Describe **three** things that Rick believes prevent human beings being good drivers.

____

____

5. Rihana's argument is all about contrasting human feelings with robotic machinery. Write down an example of this.

____

____

6. Rihana accepts that Rick makes **two** very persuasive points. What are they?

____

____

7. Rihana is almost convinced by Rick's argument. What is she not sure about?

____

____

Words that capture the reader's imagination

Strand: Language for effect

National Curriculum reference:

- discussing words and phrases that capture the reader's interest and imagination

Reading Test / Content Domain links: 2a, 2b, 2g

VICTIMS OF THE PHARAOH'S CURSE

Here is a newspaper report of what has been happening since Howard Carter and Lord Carnarvon discovered Tutankhamun's tomb. It is deliberately sensational, using very colourful, dramatic language and exaggeration, to stir the imaginations of its readers. Make a list of sensational words and phrases.

6th April 1923

CURSE OF KING TUT KILLS CARNARVON

The Tomb of Doom

Walter Klondyke reports from Cairo

Yesterday, in the opulent grandeur of the Continental-Savoy Hotel in Cairo, it has to be acknowledged that the hand of fate caught up with George Edward Stanhope Carnarvon. The gentleman who brought the Mummy's Curse into the world from the mist-ridden past has become, what I might term, its inevitable victim.

The 20th Century's sophistication might lead one to dismiss as superstitious the mysterious plans, potions and passions of an ancient people, but the finger of the pharaoh, King Tutankhamun, has, in less than six months,found the destroyer of his everlasting resting place.

Of course, the Earl is not the first. Upon opening the tomb, Egyptians who gazed, open-mouthed at its sculpted guardians with golden, snake head-dresses, were in no way surprised to hear of the death of Carter's canary by a similar serpent.

Breaking news!!!!!
At the exact second, his lordship passed away, his faithful dog, Susie, gave out a pathetic howl and died on the spot.

Those who doubt the tomb's inscription: 'Death shall come on swift wings to him that toucheth the tomb of the Pharaoh' will hope to sleep quietly in their beds.

CELEBRITY INTERVIEW

Some metaphors are so common, you'd hardly notice that they were metaphors. They have been used so much, they are what we call clichés. Here, Meena has managed to arrange an interview with the drummer of the Merekatz for the school magazine. **Underline** the metaphors / clichés.

Meena: Thank you for agreeing to this interview, Mr Ryan. I'm sure you're busy.

Jac: Call me Jac. No problem. When I heard my old school wanted to write about me, it was music to my ears. Lots of memories, of course. Good and bad, if you catch my drift: a roller-coaster of emotions. It all comes flooding back. So, fire away.

Meena: Thank you, uh... Jac. When did you first know you wanted to be a drummer?

Jac: Well, Minnie, life, as they say, is a journey, and my journey began at my mother's knee, when she would tap me on the head with a wooden spoon to the rhythm of early blues songs. Dad wasn't exactly an early bird. More a combination of night owl and couch potato, but I was the apple of his eye. So when I showed an interest in the drums, well, it was a chain reaction. First, he bought me a drum stick.

Meena: Don't you mean two drumsticks?

Jac: No, Myna. I had to wait a couple of years for the other one. What you might call a domino effect. One thing led to another. I came to a crossroads in my life. Do I get a drum or do I go on denting the saucepans, which, if you ask me, is a slippery slope to nowhere.

Meena: That must have been a difficult decision, Jac.

Jac: You hit the nail on the head there, Mona. I had a lot of bottled-up anger. The only thing to do was to bite the bullet, leave home and strike out on my own.

Meena: That must have been hard for your mother.

Jac: It surely was, Maureen. I don't like to blow my own trumpet but there's no question I broke her heart.

Meena: But things turned out well in the end.

Jac: It sure did, Michael. I met the rest of the band and it was plain sailing after that. And now, life is a breeze.

EXAMINATION BLUES

This poem describes someone's experience in an exam.

The Maths Exam

Like the sinking Titanic
My heart drowns in panic
Approaching the dark, icy room.
My lack of revision
Of basic division
Multiplies feelings of doom.

The problems with measure
Don't give me much pleasure,
Producing pulsating reactions.
Mean, median and mode,
Like a spy's secret code,
Are as clear as decimal fractions.

Sizing trapeziums
Should really be easy sums
But I'm growing hysterical.
My brain's an old boot
With cube number and root.
Is this simple shape squarish or spherical?

When I'm finding the factor
Do I need a protractor
Or is that for data-analysis?
In my estimation
This shape needs translation
But oh! My mental paralysis!

But my brain stops its fluttering
When I begin muttering
The properties of quadrilaterals
As well as the geometry
Of angles and symmetry,
Isosceles and equilaterals.

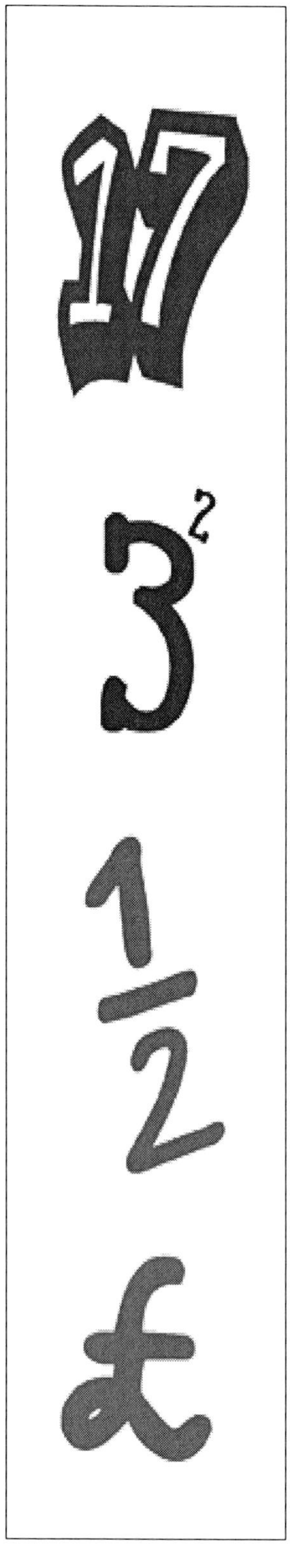

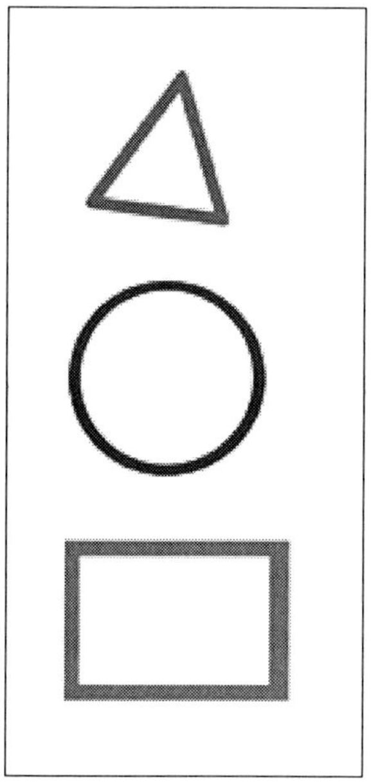

Times tables, I sense,
Give me great confidence
To tackle the hard calculations.
Line graph and pie chart
Excite me and my heart
Stops its wild palpitations.

Ratio, proportions
Induce no contortions
And I feel a buzzing sensation
Of being in charge
Of sums small and large
In this trouble-free examination.

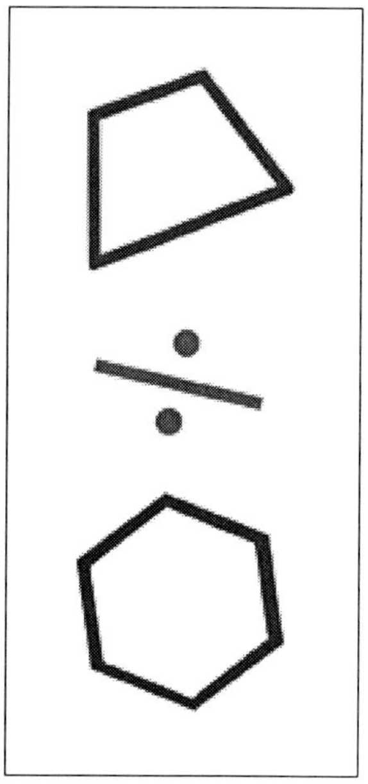

1. Write down **two** examples of simile.

2. Write down **two** examples of onomatopoeia.

3. Write down **two** examples of alliteration.

4. Find the metaphor.

THE CHASE

Personification is a special kind of metaphor in which an object or an idea is given human characteristics, for example: *The sunflowers nodded as I cycled by.* **Circle** the examples of personification in this short episode.

Every creak of a floorboard prodded my snoring guard in the shoulder, but he didn't wake up. The sleeping pills, which earlier I had surreptitiously dropped into his coffee were doing their work. As the candle flame danced around the cold, stone walls of my cell, I balanced on top of my chair on top of the table and hauled myself up to the tiny window.

Far below was the overgrown moat of this lost and long-abandoned castle, and, beyond, miles of dense forest crowded in. The trees were dressed in white and winter's grip squeezed my fingers as I pulled myself through the opening. It was a long climb down. The thorns of the ancient rose cut my hands and bits of ivy broke away to prevent my escape, but no alarm had summoned my enemy's soldiers out of the main gate. I told myself that the northerly wind was the sweet kiss of freedom and I struggled on.

The General's car was parked where he always left it. I knew that, as soon as it stirred into life, everyone would know of my escape attempt. And so it was. I hurtled into the awaiting arms of the forest with a troop of soldiers giving chase, less than half-a-mile behind. Skidding and lurching along the icy road, I reached the far side of the ridge. Here, the trees thinned and a valley bathed itself in moonlight. That's when the car slowed to a crawl, and, out of petrol, the engine coughed its last.

My dream was not going to die. I scrambled down the gentle slope. Though the wind howled, I could still hear the General's voice echoing across the snowy landscape: "Run as fast as you can! Death will catch you up!"

I smiled. Life had slapped him in the face and he did not like it. I moved on to the city that keeps its secrets. Safe for now.

A TALENT FOR TALKING

The judges of this talent show have a way with words. Read what they have to say.

The first contestant was one in a million. Her voice was like a nightingale sitting on the wing of an angel. But talent is one thing. If she wants to do anything with it, she'll have to work harder than Noah works on his quiff. If she fails in the final round, she needs to know that future success is just a performance away. I'd say that music is food and water to this girl.

As the great Bob Marley said: when the music hits you, you feel no pain. But listening to the second contestant was like listening to a poet reciting words to his sweetheart. This guy has a voice that could make the rocks weep tears of joy. It's as if he's captured the sun's brilliance and worked on it and worked on it until it is pure energy. He's one-of-a-kind.

My choice is No. 4. I hope he'll go through. He has a unique sound: it's dark chocolate with more chocolate on top. My only concern is that he thinks that talent is all you need. You have to work at it. After all, what's the use of a camel in the snow – if you get my drift? But for now, I'd say his music shapes the air into exquisite sculptures.

Listening to the other judges, you'd think they were hearing something out of the ordinary. I've heard better sounds scraping jam on my toast. Talent is a window in a palace and No. 3 has been shining it tirelessly. The rendition of her song cleansed my dusty soul. She is the icing on the cake, the rose among the nettles, the honey in my porridge.

1. Ricky uses the phrase **something out of the ordinary**. The other three judges use words and phrases that mean something similar. What are they?

____

____

____

2. Write down similes used by Kitty and Noah.

____

____

3. Write down the examples of personification used by Noah and Carrie.

____

____

4. Carrie uses two metaphors. What are they?

____

____

5. Ricky goes overboard with his metaphors. Write down **two** of them.

____

____

6. They all have something similar to say about talent. What is it?

____

7. Both Kitty and Ricky use colourful comparisons to tease their fellow judges and their choice of contestants. What do they say?

____

____

Explaining how words and phrases enhance meaning

Strand: Language for effect

National Curriculum reference:

- discussing words and phrases that capture the reader's interest and imagination

Reading Test / Content Domain links: 2a, 2b, 2g

WORDS FOR SALE

You find all sorts of things for sale on the web as well as on community noticeboards. Here are some. Decide whether the chosen words and phrases are used to inform or to persuade.

The Height of Style

Luxuriate in 21st Century skyscraper living experience in this delightful 12th floor apartment with panoramic views of London. Exquisite accommodation, furnished to the highest standard you deserve. Ideal for business or relaxing. Treat yourself to shopping frenzy only five minutes away at the Wherewithal Mall. Leave your email for prices.

Blue Fronted Amazon Parrot

Blue Fronted Amazon Parrot called Andrew for sale to kind owner as I've got to leave the country double-quick. He's a beautiful specimen. Hand-reared, very friendly and will talk to anybody. He has an excellent vocabulary, including: 'peek-a-boo, what are you up to my lad?' and 'the money's stashed under the bed'. Quite a sense of humour. £5 for a quick sale, no questions asked.

PIE PARADISE

Visit Pie Paradise and partake of the premium pies of the planet. Sweet or savoury, pineapple or pork, we have a pie that will fit you perfectly. Or sign up now to our heavenly list of international fans. Now don't forget – Put Away a Pie Paradise Pie Today!

Stanley's Sheds

The Sumo is our most popular shed. Compact on the outside, deceptively wide on the inside, you'll find that it is spacious enough to store a ladder, your lawnmower and a large bag of spuds. We promise you will not be disappointed. Our prices include all screws and a box of plasters for self-assembly. Money-back guarantee if you're unable to fit an average sized Japanese wrestler in there as well.

SOCK HEAVEN

Have you been standing around all day? Is that your feet I hear complaining? If so, TREAT THE FEET straightaway to a visit from one of our Sock Heaven angels. Using our unique, ultra-safe, laser technology, your own personal sock angel will produce a masterpiece in silky softness, made-to-measure to fit your tootsies no matter what shape they are. Call now for an estimate.

Now **tick** the box to show whether a word or phrase is intended to inform or to persuade. Some may be both.

word or phrase	informative	persuasive
The Height of Style		
Blue Fronted Amazon Parrot		
Pie Paradise		
Sock Heaven		
delightful		
12th floor apartment		
Exquisite accommodation		
the highest standard you deserve		
Ideal for business or relaxing		
I've got to leave the country		
beautiful specimen		
hand-reared		
very friendly		
will talk to anybody		
£5 for a quick sale		
the premium pies of the planet		
sweet or savoury		
a pie that will fit you perfectly		
our most popular shed		
deceptively wide on the inside		
you will not be disappointed		
Is that your feet I hear complaining?		
Treat the Feet		
Sock Heaven angels		
ultra-safe laser technology		
a masterpiece in silky softness		
Call now for an estimate		

MAD ABOUT METAPHORS

Here is a poem packed full of metaphors, in which one object, action or event is compared to another without the use of the words 'like' or 'as'.

Night Boat From Thebes

when the sun is a sigh across the back
of a slumbering beast
shadow night limps with a bent-stick moon
slowly from the east
hovering river kings crowd the air hungry
to spear unwitting fish
a rabble of mosquitoes jostle to feast on
its human dish
the pharaoh awaits the knot of our hands
and shoulders of brother slaves
to start his blind journey to the house of
his father - our eyes must be caves
for we are on Earth to nurse his sail and
cradle his oar
our very breath belongs to he who needs
it no more
but another sapling is ready to grow in the
sand and draw tears from the sky
and dance to the tune of the slave's lullaby

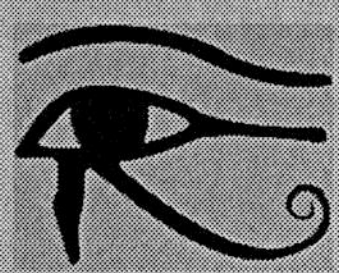

Now underline the metaphors, then answer the questions on the next page.

1. Who is the narrator?

____

2. What time of day is it when the narrator is speaking?

____

3. What is the **slumbering beast**?

____

4. A crescent moon is in the sky. How do you know?

____

5. What are the **hovering river kings**?

____

6. The words **rabble** and **jostle** are used to describe the mosquitoes. Why are these words appropriate?

____

____

7. Although slaves play an important part, they are not permitted to watch. How do you know?

____

8. What two words tell us the slaves' work must be done as silently and respectfully as possible?

____________________ ____________________

9. Who or what is **another sapling ... ready to grow in the sand**?

____

10. What are **tears from the sky**?

____

Themes and conventions

Strand: Themes and conventions

National Curriculum reference:

- identifying themes and conventions in a wide range of books

Reading Test / Content Domain links: 2a, 2b, 2c, 2f, 2g

SUPERHEROES

Here is a description of an ordinary day in the lives of two superheroes.

05:00 Woken by dawn chorus and The Beak demanding breakfast. It seems to me a superhero's assistant should be able to assemble its own muesli.

05:30 Usual morning routine: checked my sonar-disruptor, metal creepers and communication device to my personal army of paralysing ants.

06:45 Left Hollowoak in response to ground rumbling – I could feel it among the roots. My treetop-hopping seems to get faster by the day. Reached Snake Mountain in seconds. I could see Reptilion had his hands full, so I bounded up to the edge of the crater.

07:00 Switched on the receiver on the sonar disruptor to analyse the sounds. Whose voice should I hear but the Shrieker – the one creature who recognises the retinas of Iona Marshall. He knows how to turn my own ants on me. Certain death!

08:00 Our plan's got to work. Reptilion's dream-zapper slows the Shrieker down just long enough to immobilise him with my metal creepers. Job done!

06:30 I don't know how Jekko learnt to talk and keep up with emerging news stories. Anyway, he's a gecko in a million. He alerted me to the rumbling taking place under Snake Mountain. Could be an earth tremor. Maybe the old volcano was wakening up. Could be something much more sinister.

06:45 Landed the Repwing at the foothills and found local people totally zombified. It didn't take much to put them out of action with my dream-zapper. Maybe I'd get more sleep if I tried it on myself. Too much echoing noise in the sewers.

07:00 Jekko tells me it isn't the tectonic plates that are at work; it's machinery.

07:15 This is the Shrieker's personal invitation to me. He wants to unmask me as Professor Dury. My slime detector shows high amounts of biridin. Better be careful. Don't want to waste away. Time to change shape.

8:00 FaunaFlora works at the speed of light and has him trussed up. Dream-zapper should slow down his memory too.

Now check the information in the text to complete the database below.

SuperHero database		
Feature	**FaunaFlora**	**Reptilion**
sidekick / assistant		
special abilities		
special gadgets (and what do they do?)		
vehicle / means of transport		
secret headquarters		
secret identity		
weaknesses		
arch enemy (and what are they able to do?)		

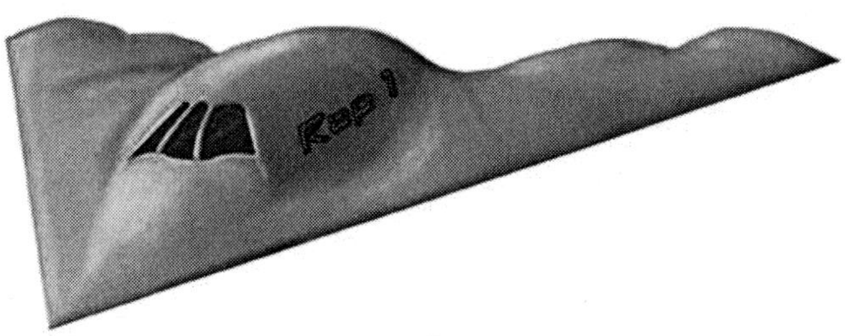

ANOTHER WORLD

Science fiction is often set in another world or a future version of our world after some global crisis. There, you will find contact with alien life forms, artificial intelligence, a focus on one or two survivors, conflict involving outlandish weapons or strange vehicles – all of which is often described in scientific-sounding or alien language. Read the following extract and make a note of some of these features.

The Sands of Zylon 7

A silver dust cloud moving across the far horizon heralded the approach of a GravX Ion Disruptor. It wasn't entirely unexpected. The osmium-based life forms known as Krish would have been alerted the moment we ruptured their robotzoid guard's security shield. What we didn't expect to find was a photon-converter among the wreckage of robotic wiring and DNA replication. We could do some major discolouration with that in our possession. As Z'bella, a captured olian from the planet Garsz, pointed out by means of her linguaphon implant, our escape plan had just turned into a means of shutting down Tereer, the Krish's evil empire.

Zylon 7, this artificial moon covered in silver dust, orbited Tereer to provide the Krish with the reflected light and energy to power their devastating voyages throughout space. Z'bella and I – a solitary Ichobi so far from my home in the Outer Tsapudi region and taken prisoner sixteen astral years ago – we might now have the means of standing in their way.

The GravX pulled up in a shower of silver beside the bits and pieces of the neutralised robotzoid guard. One of the Krish reluctantly slid out of the transporter, his weight just a little too much for the moon's gravitational pull. His luminous body quivered and his eyes spun round his head as he kicked the guard's metal head. We hoped that covering as much of ourselves in the granules of silver that we shovelled every Sagittarian day would be camouflage enough. But a trickle of grains alerted the seven-legged Krish, who turned quickly. It was now or never.

Z'bella plugged the photon-converter into her neuron outlet and scanned the whole area. Light drained from Zylon 7. A freezing wind swept our dark desert. And Tereer slowly was lost in shadow, until, moments later, as energy systems broke down, it exploded into nothingness.

Making comparisons

Strand: Make comparisons within the text

National Curriculum reference:

- making comparisons within and across books

Reading Test / Content Domain links: 2a, 2b, 2c, 2d, 2f, 2g, 2h

RESTAURANT REVIEWS

Compare these two quite different reviews of the same restaurant, representing two contrasting experiences.

pie-adviser

Pete's Pie Paradise ***** 366 reviews

Review Highlights

"... stepped inside the gates of Eden ..."

***** 14 August 2015

Since the Neanderthal age, when an early caveman found that someone had run off with his mammoth pie, brave men and women have travelled the four corners of the Earth in search of the perfect pie. Chefs at the beck and call of kings and queens, emperors and presidents have laboured night and day, willing to sell their souls in exchange for the secret of ultimate crustiness and heavenly filling. My own personal quest came to an end when I stepped inside the gates of Eden that are the doors of Pete's Pie Paradise. Not only are the staff charming angels, this restaurant, like no other, is the stuff of pie dreams. Every baking product is a masterpiece worthy of a place of honour in the country's finest art gallery. One bite will have you enslaved for life. Whether you choose savoury, dessert or both, you'll find nothing better the world over.

"... still glued in its own gravy ..."

* 23 September 2015

Picture the atmosphere inside a derelict caravan abandoned in a farmer's field. The cows and sheep have recently been shown the door. Add to that a poorly-paid, depressed, overworked staff trained at the Wayward Vagabond School for Rude Waiters, and you have an image of what nightmare awaits you at the so-called Paradise provided by Pete. It's possible I made the wrong choice from the menu, but my rhubarb and squid pie came straight out of the freezer still glued in its own gravy to the plate. When I complained, the waiter kicked it all the way back to the kitchen and, thankfully, didn't return until it was time to pay the bill. Mathematics was not my strong point at school, but one and one do not make three! My wife and I scurried out as fast as we could. Visit Pete's Palace of Perfectly Poisonous Pies at your own peril!

Both reviews – the 5* and the 1* – contain colourful images. Contrast the images used to describe the atmosphere inside the restaurant, the staff, the food and the bill.

*****	*

Write down any other examples of criticisms or praise here:

AN ECLIPSE OF THE SUN

Here are two different pieces of writing in different styles. One is **formal** – official advice to schools about how to experience a solar eclipse safely. The other is **informal** – the diary entry of someone who has had direct experience of an eclipse.

PRIMARY SAFETY: ADVISORY SERVICE

SOLAR ECLIPSE

An eclipse of the sun is a natural event, though a full eclipse seen from the British Isles is quite rare. It happens when the Moon, in its orbit around our planet, passes between the Earth and the Sun. The sky darkens much more quickly than it does during the normal course of an ordinary day, creating a twilight effect. You might experience birds starting to sing as if it were dawn or early evening and flowers are often seen to close. Further background information is available from the department's website.

This will be a fairly unique experience in the lives of your pupils. Schools are encouraged to provide adequate supervision, so that children may witness the phenomenon in safety.

A WORD OF WARNING

Looking directly at the sun can result in permanent damage to the eyes and reliable protection should be worn. Pupils must be supervised at all times.

[02/03/2015]

Friday 20 th March 2015

Dear Diary,

Miss Jones took us to catch sight of the moon getting in the way of the sun. It blocked the sunshine and Miss told us it was, like, a normal thing that happened now and again. It got like bedtime and the birds all started twittering like it was time for breakfast. Miss said, if you look straight at it, your eyeballs'll bulge or something, so I put on the funny specs and it was great! My friend, Toby, said he wasn't going to look stupid wearing them, so Miss sent him inside, because she couldn't keep an eye on everybody, and that's how he lost out on the whole amazing thing.

Spot the differences! Compare the two texts and, in the table below. Pick out as many things as you can find that are different in these two pieces of writing.

formal	informal

YEAR 6 TESTS

<u>PLEASE NOTE:</u>

The digital version also contains the book and tests filed separately for printing. A full answer version and colour digital versions of the book and tests are also included.

The raw score/scaled score conversion charts are also supplied.

Strand: Range of texts

National Curriculum objectives:

- [listening to and] discussing a wide range of fiction, poetry, plays, non-fiction and reference books or textbooks
- reading books that are structured in different ways and reading for a range of purposes
- increasing their familiarity with a wide range of books, including fairy stories, myths and legends [and retelling some of these orally]

Reading Test / Content Domain links: 2a, 2b, 2c, 2d, 2e, 2f, 2g

A note about the tests:

The KS2 English Reading Test Framework 2016 (table 9) sets out the proportion of marks for each domain, with the higher percentages given to **retrieving and recording information** and **making inferences**. This is reflected in the test questions presented here.

Year 6 Reading Comprehension - Test Admin Guidance

Before Starting the Test

Explain to the children that the questions require different kinds of answers.

- The space for the answer shows the type of answer required. Some questions require a one word/short answer and others require a longer answer.
- For some questions, a different type of answer is required e.g. circling/ticking an answer or joining two items together with a line.
- The number underneath the line on the right-hand side of each question indicates how many marks there are for each question.

Timing

Pupils should take approximately 60 minutes to complete these tests. The primary purpose of these tests is to diagnose children's strengths and weaknesses, so allow longer if necessary. If appropriate, the test can be stopped and re-started as long as pupils do not have a chance to share/discuss the test content.

Equipment

Each pupil will need a pencil or pen.

A rubber can be used but crossing out is preferable as long as answers remain legible.

Assistance

General instructions on the test papers may be read to children. Instructions may also be re-phrased as long as no inappropriate assistance is given.

In Year 6, it may be appropriate for some children to read the texts and questions aloud if this is part of normal classroom practice. This should happen in a different room than children completing the tests silently.

Children with Special Needs or Disabilities

If children need specific kinds of assistance, equipment or environment to complete the tests, this should be provided as long as it is part of normal classroom practice.

HeadStart
primary

YEAR 6

Reading Booklet

Scaled Score TEST A

Buffalo Bill's Wild West

The Industrial Revolution

Let Them Eat Cake

CONTENTS

HeadStart primary

BUFFALO BILL'S WILD WEST

EARLY DAYS:

Although born in Iowa, William spent much of his early life in Kansas, having to find work at the age of eleven when his father died. Three years later, he was working as a rider for the Pony Express: a mail service, using a relay of horseback riders, who, in ten days, were able to deliver messages the 3000-plus miles from the Atlantic coast of America to California on the Pacific.

Between 1863 and 1865, he fought in the American Civil War. Later, during what was known as the Plains Wars between the Native Americans and the US government, he became a scout, receiving the Medal of Honour in 1872. During this time, he had hunted bison as well (also known as buffalo) to provide food for the army. This is how he got his nickname. (Later, he would claim to have had many jobs, including trapper, goldminer, wagon-master, stagecoach driver and hotel manager. No one is sure if this is true. He might have been trying to make his life sound more interesting.)

BUFFALO BILL

Real name: William Frederick Cody
Born: 26th February 1846 in Le Claire, Iowa, USA
Died: 10th January 1917

THE FIRST AMERICAN CELEBRITY:

In 1883, Cody created 'Buffalo Bill's Wild West', a circus-like show that toured the country. This massively popular attraction included sharp-shooting by Annie Oakley, another celebrity at the time; re-enactments of the Pony Express; rodeo skills; and the dramatisation of the rescue of white settlers or wagon trains under attack by Native Americans.

It is worth noting that the Native Americans he fought during the Plains Wars – the Lakota, members of the Sioux Nation – were also part of his Wild West show. As a frontier scout, he had great respect for Native Americans and supported their rights. By employing them in his show, he believed he was offering them a chance to improve their lives. He is quoted as saying, 'Every Indian outbreak that I have ever known has resulted from broken promises and broken treaties by the government.'

In 1887, Buffalo Bill brought his show to Britain in order to play in front of Queen Victoria to celebrate her Jubilee (50 years on the throne). He visited Europe several times, his final tour reaching as far as Eastern Europe as well as many towns and cities in the UK.

THE INDUSTRIAL REVOLUTION

Queen Victoria ruled from 1837 until 1901. During that time, Britain changed from being, on the whole, a rural society to the most advanced industrialised country in the world. Huge numbers of people, who had worked on farms or in **cottage industries**, such as spinning and weaving, lace-making and furniture-making, moved to the cities to live and work. If you were wealthy enough, you might be able to have a ride in one of the very first cars, have your photograph taken or have electric lights in your home. If you were poor, you would live in a single room with, possibly, ten other family members and work very long hours in a factory.

'I started at Bradford Mill when I was nine and had to carry Benjamin, who was five then and often still asleep. We worked from six in the morning till ten or eleven at night."

Charles Dickens was (and still is) a very successful writer, whose novels describe the terrible lives of the poor in Britain. Born in 1812, he died in 1870 an internationally famous author. Throughout the world, he is known as an outspoken critic of living conditions in Victorian society.

He wanted to see better conditions in factories, especially for children, who, he believed, needed education to help them avoid the risks of the terrible, disease-ridden and often criminal life of the slums.

He knew something of what life was like for poor people. When he was 12 years old, his own father was sent to prison for six months for not paying his bills. This meant that Charles had to find work in a dirty, noisy and dangerous factory. (Factories were known as *dark satanic mills.*) He would use this experience later in his stories.

Oliver Twist was published the same year as Victoria came to the throne. It is the story of an orphan boy who, after a difficult time in a workhouse – a prison-like home for poor people with no work – ends up in a criminal gang learning to be a pickpocket.

LET THEM EAT CAKE

A cake competition is being held at Panettone School for Girls and Boys. Read below some of the experiences of a few of the contestants.

For me, it's – like - the major event of the year. Wanna know why? I'll tell you why. It means so much. Maybe that's why the worst time was trying to sleep the night before. I kept dreaming of silver foxes made of icing running off with my marzipan bunnies.

Tarte Tatin. It's French, you know. An inverted fruit pie without the crust on top. The story goes that it was invented by mistake when someone threw apples into a pan, forgetting to put the pastry in first. Anyway, the Tatin sisters made it in the Hotel Tatin southwest of Paris, in a little town my mother comes from. She'll be really pleased when I tell her the results.

I decided to make stollen. You know, a German Christmas cake. Dad said he was looking forward to anything left over after my schoolmates had a go at demolishing it. I had everything ready: dried fruit, nuts, cinnamon. I turned round for the marzipan and it was gone! Well, it didn't run off by itself, did it? It was stolen!

I thought I'd give myself a head start. Panettone – it's the name of the school. The judges were bound to like that connection. Cake and school – same name! But I was getting so hungry! When the starting buzzer went, my stomach rumbled loudly. I stared at the almonds and thought: what do I do now? D'you know what I did?

HeadStart primary

Reading Comprehension

YEAR 6

Scaled Score TEST A

ANSWER BOOKLET

Name: ....

Class: ....

Date: ....

Raw Score .... /50

Scaled Score ....

The following questions are about *BUFFALO BILL'S WILD WEST* (Page 1)

1. Which **two** American states were part of William Cody's childhood?

   1. ....

   2. ....

   2 marks

2. How old was William when he went to work for the Pony Express?

   ....

   1 mark

3. How long did it take the Pony Express's relay system of riders to deliver letters coast to coast?

   ....

   1 mark

4. Cody fought in **two** wars. What were they?

   1. ....

   2. ....

   2 marks

5. What was his job when he received the Medal of Honour?

   ....

   1 mark

6. How did Cody come to be nicknamed Buffalo Bill?

   ....

   ....

   ....

   1 mark

Page Total

7. Cody said that he had done many different jobs.

Write down **three** jobs, apart from scout and hunter, that he said he did.

1. ....

2. ....

3. ....

2 marks

8. When was Buffalo Bill's Wild West created?

....

1 mark

9. How did he become a celebrity?

....

....

1 mark

10. Describe **three** attractions that were associated with the show.

1. ....

2. ....

3. ....

....

3 marks

11. What was the name of the Native Americans who were in his show?

....

1 mark

12. Why was it possible for Buffalo Bill and the Native Americans to work together, despite being on opposite sides during the Plains Wars?

Write down **three reasons**.

1. ....

....

2. ....

....

3. ....

....

3 marks

13. What special occasion brought Buffalo Bill's show to Britain?

....

1 mark

14. What feature does this text contain that tells you this is a biography?

....

1 mark

15. Why has some biographical information been placed inside a box?

....

1 mark

End of questions about
BUFFALO BILL'S WILD WEST

Page Total

The following questions are about ***THE INDUSTRIAL REVOLUTION*** (Page 2)

1. The changes that took place in Britain during the reign of Queen Victoria affected huge numbers of people. What happened?

....

....

2 marks

2. **Circle** the word that is similar in meaning to **on the whole**.

mainly **always** **rarely**

1 mark

3. What is the phrase used to describe people weaving and making lace, etc. at home?

....

1 mark

4. Using the information given, how was life different for the rich and the poor? **Draw lines** matching rich and poor people to their lives.

rich	**lived in a single room**
	had electric lights
poor	**rode in cars**
	worked in factories

2 marks

Page Total

5. As well as new machinery that could make things faster, find in the text another thing that was invented in Victorian times. **Tick one**.

furniture ☐

camera ☐

electric car ☐

1 mark

6. Look at the quotation that begins: **'I started at Bradford Mill...'**

What sort of person do you think said this?

....

1 mark

7. How do you know five-year-old Benjamin also had to work in the factory?

....

1 mark

8. Dickens wanted to see changes in the life of the poor. He is described as **outspoken**. What does this mean? **Tick one**.

He gave lots of speeches in public. ☐

He wasn't worried about speaking his mind. ☐

Other people spoke louder than him. ☐

1 mark

9 Living in Victorian slums put children at risk.

The text describes **two** terrible things they were likely to suffer.

What were they?

1. ....

2. ....

2 marks

10 Something happened in the early life of Dickens and his family that influenced what he later put into his stories. What was it?

....

....

....

2 marks

11 In what year was *Oliver Twist* published?

....

1 mark

12 *Oliver Twist* is the story of an orphan who had no work.

This led him to a sad and difficult life.

Write down **two** things that happened to him.

1. ....

....

2. ....

....

2 marks

End of questions about
THE INDUSTRIAL REVOLUTION

Page Total

The following questions are about ***LET THEM EAT CAKE*** (Page 3)

1. Find **two** examples of informal speech.

1. ....

2. ....

1 mark

2. **Circle** the word or phrase that is similar in meaning to **inverted**.

microwaved | **upside-down** | **baked in the oven**

1 mark

3. What is Sophie mainly talking about? **Tick one**.

The competition is a major event. ☐

Trying to sleep is the hardest bit. ☐

She had strange dreams. ☐

1 mark

4. Which cake was originally made in a hotel in France?

....

1 mark

5. Ashley says, "**I thought I'd give myself a head start.**"

He hopes that, by making a cake called panettone, he will impress the judges. Why?

....

....

....

2 marks

6. Who are the **two** contestants who were planning to have marzipan among their ingredients?

1. ....

2. ....

1 mark

7. Ashley says, "**I stared at the almonds and thought: what do I do now? D'you know what I did?**"

What do you think he did?

....

....

1 mark

8. The writer has included some questions in the speech bubbles of some of the contestants. What effect does this have on the reader?

....

....

1 mark

9 Describe how Sammy's cake might look after his schoolmates

'**...have a go at demolishing it.**'

....

....

1 mark

10 Who do you think won the cake competition, and how do you know?

....

....

1 mark

End of questions about
LET THEM EAT CAKE

End of TEST A

Page Total

HeadStart
primary

YEAR 6

Reading Booklet

Scaled Score TEST B

The Wild-Life Friendly Garden

The Artist's Garden

Micro-Organisms

CONTENTS

HeadStart primary

THE WILDLIFE-FRIENDLY GARDEN

If we can show that we're able to manage the project from beginning to end, our headteacher has agreed to let Year 6 create a wildlife garden. Wow!

So, first thing we did was look at the school grounds and decide on the most suitable area. Here are our plans and a few notes. Hope Mrs Brown's impressed.

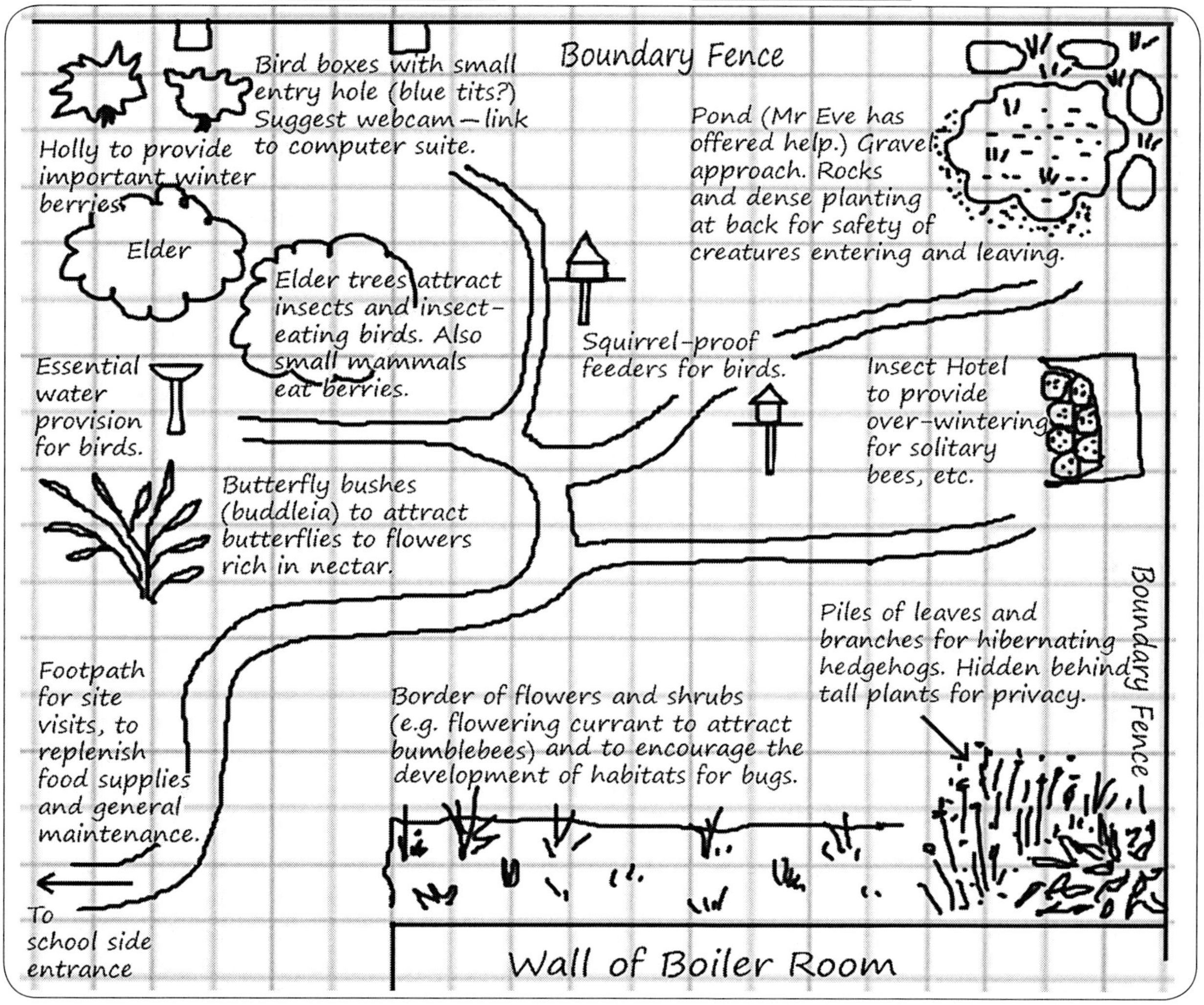

Notes:
Mrs B suggests signs to advise holly berries are mildly poisonous. Yrs 3 & 4 need supervision. Same for people observing pond life habitat. Jonah's dad, Mr Eve the builder, has offered gravel + rubber liner for pond. In talks with local garden centre for free plants past their best. Might Yr 5 make bird boxes – DT project? Also bird feeders? Mr Ramesh in 5A says maybe. Katya is writing piece for school newsletter to encourage parent volunteers to help with manual work. (Baz has already volunteered his parents!) Miss Flint to set up bird-box webcam. Still to do: logs etc. for insect hotel, material for path, large natural rocks for pond. Mr Jones sees art potential.

THE ARTIST'S GARDEN

BEST-SELLING GIVERNY TOURS

BOOK ONLINE NOW from £62

Claude Monet

Every day from 28th March – 1st November your personal guide is available to provide a tour of Monet's beautiful garden at Giverny, the setting that inspired so many of his brilliant paintings.

- ✓ **Ticket includes entrance to Monet's home and garden**
- ✓ **Gain an insight into the art and family life of Monet**
- ✓ **Admire the lily pond that inspired so many of his paintings**
- ✓ **Tour includes an English-speaking guide**

This delightful, relaxing 5-star tour will whisk you away from the hubbub of Paris to the peaceful village, where Monet – a green-fingered gardener as well as a famous painter – created the glorious garden, which was the subject of so many of his amazing masterpieces. Your well-informed guide will delve into the past to help you enter the picture of Monet's life. Stand and admire his house with its famous pink façade and green shutters. Stroll, as he did, among the colourful flowerbeds. Pause to absorb the beauty of the climbing plants. Witness for yourself the Japanese footbridge and the joyful sight of the water-lily pond. Often referred to as the 'Painter of Light', Monet would paint the same landscape at different times of day in order to capture changes in the light in the morning, afternoon and evening.

CHECK AVAILABILITY

CUSTOMER REVIEWS

★★★★★

Gorgeous, unforgettable experience like stepping into another world. We loved the souvenir shop. Would recommend this... *K. James, Derby*

★★★★

Garden and house were amazing but not the place for two lively six year-olds. Unfortunately, it poured that day... *B. Johnson, London*

FAQs

How long is the visit?
Average: 1 hr 15 min depending how long visitors wish to admire the view.

Is Monet's house part of the tour?
Guides are not allowed inside but you can visit on your own.

Can I bring my dog?
Dogs and other pets are not permitted.

Can I bring my children?
Yes, if accompanied by a responsible adult. They must remain calm and respect the premises and other visitors.

Can I have a picnic in the garden?
Picnics are not allowed.

Is photography allowed?
Only from designated walkways.

Is there wheelchair access?
Yes, though it is not part of the guide's role to push the wheelchair.

What if I cancel?
Money will be refunded up to 30 days before the tour, but not afterwards.

MICRO-ORGANISMS

Our understanding of good and bad micro-organisms has increased, thanks to the scientific research of the medical pioneers listed in these pages from a book on the history of medicine.

The Battle Against Bacteria

Edward Jenner (1749 – 1823)

During the 18th century, small pox replaced the plague as the biggest killer disease in Europe. Babies and young children were particularly vulnerable. The pioneering work of Jenner, however, a doctor in Gloucestershire, changed all that. He noticed that those, such as milkmaids, working with cows often caught cowpox – a minor illness – and became immune to smallpox. This led him to the idea of vaccination using cowpox serum. It was a success.

Louis Pasteur (1822 – 1895)

Louis Pasteur was a French chemist who showed that germs present in the air led to disease. Working for a wine company whose wine was turning sour, he was able to show that this was due to germs, which were visible under a microscope. His process of killing germs by boiling the wine then cooling it is what we call pasteurisation. Like Jenner, he developed vaccinations for a variety of diseases and advised that surgeons' instruments should be boiled before operations.

Sir Alexander Fleming (1881 – 1955)

Alexander Fleming was a captain in the Army Medical Corps during the First World War, where he witnessed how frequently soldiers died from simple infections. In 1928, while cleaning some Petri dishes, he noticed that mould had started to grow on one of them, killing some bacteria alongside it. (It was similar to the blue mould that grows on bread.) He named it penicillin. It has since been used to treat many infections that are harmful to humans.

Florence Nightingale (1820 – 1910)

In 1854, Florence Nightingale and 38 other nurses travelled to Scutari to the military hospital to tend those wounded in the Crimean War. Many of the soldiers were dying, not of battle-inflicted injuries, but because of infections and poor sanitation. By improving hygiene and providing the men with fresh food, she reduced the death rate from 60% to just over 2% by the spring of 1855. Known as the 'Lady with the Lamp', she brought about many changes in hospitals.

HeadStart primary

Reading Comprehension

YEAR 6

Scaled Score TEST B

ANSWER BOOKLET

Name: ....

Class: ....

Date: ....

Raw Score .... /50

Scaled Score ....

The following questions are about ***THE WILD-LIFE FRIENDLY GARDEN*** (Page 1)

1 What is the headteacher's name?

.... 1 mark

2 In the **Notes** box, what does **mildly** mean in the phrase: **holly berries are mildly poisonous**?

Tick one.

slightly ☐

dangerously ☐

always ☐

1 mark

3 Not all the information in the **Notes** box is written as complete sentences. Sometimes words are missed out.

Write down **two** examples of notes that are not complete sentences.

1. ....

2. ....

2 marks

4 Why do you think Mrs B has suggested children in Years 3 and 4 need supervision? **Tick one.**

children might scare the wildlife ☐

children might eat holly berries ☐

children might climb on the fence ☐

1 mark

5 How might **rocks and dense planting** make it safer for creatures like newts and frogs entering and leaving the pond? **Tick one**.

they would keep dry if it rained ☐

they would have plants to eat ☐

they would be safe from predators ☐

1 mark

6 What is meant by **gravel approach**? **Tick one**.

gravel for the pond has been delivered ☐

gravel placed at front edge of the pond ☐

a source of gravel has been found ☐

1 mark

7 What are the **three** benefits to wildlife of elder trees?

1. ....

2. ....

3. ....

2 marks

8 Some habitats have been planned for hibernating.

Name the **two** animals which would benefit.

1. ....

2. ....

1 mark

9 Name **two** plants that will provide berries.

1. ....

2. ....

1 mark

10 Why is the buddleia called the Butterfly Bush?

....

1 mark

11 What do you think the webcam will show?

....

....

1 mark

12 What is the name of the boy whose father will provide building materials?

....

1 mark

13 **Baz has already volunteered his parents!** Why has this sentence been given an exclamation mark?

....

....

....

1 mark

14 On the map, there is a **footpath for site visits, to replenish food supplies. . .**

What does **replenish** mean here? **Tick one**.

refill ☐

remove ☐

measure ☐

1 mark

15 **Three** materials are still needed. What are they and what part will they play in the wildlife garden?

1. ....

....

2. ....

....

3. ....

....

3 marks

16 There are some clues in the **Notes** to suggest that some school subjects could benefit from having a wildlife garden.

Describe **three** school subjects, explaining how the garden could be a useful resource.

school subject	How would the garden be useful?
....	....
....	....
....	....

3 marks

End of questions about
THE WILD-LIFE FRIENDLY GARDEN

The following questions are about ***THE ARTIST'S GARDEN*** (Page 2)

1. Pick out one feature that tells you this is a web page.

   .... 1 mark

2. Who is available to give visitors a tour of the garden?

   .... 1 mark

3. Why has the length of the tour been given as an average?

   .... 1 mark

4. Does the ticket include being able to look inside Monet's house?

   .... 1 mark

5. What do you think would happen if you came to have a picnic?

   .... 1 mark

6. Monet's garden is described as **beautiful**.

   Find and write down **three** other phrases used to make the garden sound attractive to visitors.

   1. ....

   2. ....

   3. .... 3 marks

Page Total

7 The text contains some words and phrases that are **facts**.

Others are **opinions**.

Decide whether the following words and phrases are **facts** or **opinions** and **put a tick in the correct box**.

words or phrases	fact	opinion
best-selling		
Every day from 28th March - 1st November		
delightful, relaxing 5-star tour		
his amazing masterpieces		

2 marks

8 Gardeners are sometimes described as **green-fingered**.

Why do you think this is? **Tick one** sentence.

They are very messy. ☐

They are very good at gardening. ☐

They get green paint on their fingers. ☐

1 mark

9 **Stand and admire his house...**

Why does this phrase sound like instructions?

....

1 mark

10 Monet is described as the **Painter of Light**.

What was special about how he painted?

....

....

1 mark

11 What are the clues that suggest it may not be the right place for lively children?

....

....

2 marks

12 A customer review states, **'like stepping into another world'.**

Find a similar phrase in the text.

....

1 mark

13 **Tick one** word or phrase that is similar in meaning to **unforgettable**.

easily forgotten ☐

dramatic ☐

memorable ☐

1 mark

End of questions about
THE ARTIST'S GARDEN

The following questions are about ***MICRO-ORGANISMS*** (Page 3)

1 In the section on Edward Jenner, find a word that means **'unprotected'**.

....

1 mark

2 What was Edward Jenner's occupation?

....

1 mark

3 What was it about Alexander Fleming's army experience that made him interested in researching germs?

....

....

1 mark

4 Why do you think Louis Pasteur recommended boiling instruments before operations?

....

....

2 marks

5 Who made a chance discovery?

....

1 mark

Page Total

6 In the sections on Alexander Fleming and Florence Nightingale, there is a **main idea** common to both.

Tick which **one** you think is correct.

sanitary conditions are important ☐

soldiers were dying of infection ☐

penicillin kills germs ☐

1 mark

7 Where was the military hospital in which Florence Nightingale did her work?

....

1 mark

8 Who carried on some of the work begun by Jenner?

....

1 mark

9 How is the mould described that led to the development of penicillin?

....

1 mark

10 **Two** things improved the lives of soldiers wounded in the Crimean War. What were they?

1. ....

2. ....

1 mark

End of questions about
MICRO-ORGANISMS

End of TEST B

Page Total

HeadStart
primary

YEAR 6

Reading Booklet

Scaled Score TEST C

The Mystery of the Mary Celeste

The Ghost Ship

The Unsinkable Titanic

Narrow Escape

CONTENTS

HeadStart primary

THE MYSTERY OF THE MARY CELESTE

Originally called the Amazon, but renamed in 1868 by a new owner, the **Mary Celeste** was a type of merchant ship known as a brigantine, built to transport goods across the Atlantic. It was launched in 1861. In 1872, it was found off the Azores Islands (500 miles from Portugal) with no one on board and its cargo untouched. The investigation that followed came up with no explanation.

The Ghost Ship

In January 1884, Arthur Conan Doyle, the creator of Sherlock Holmes, wrote a short story inspired by the Mary Celeste incident. In his story, he called the ship the **Marie Celeste**. Passengers started a mutiny against the captain and abandoned the vessel on their way to Africa. Doyle did not think the newspapers would treat his story as fact.

As captain of the vessel that discovered the Mary Celeste on December 4, in the year of our Lord 1872, I would, in sound mind and body, make the following statement. For it is my intention to dispel the myths and falsehoods that have been written in the newspapers and spread by word of mouth in every tavern in the country.

The facts are these:
When we boarded the brigantine – records show that it had set sail from New York on its way to Genoa – there was no one on board and one lifeboat was missing. Its cargo of fuel remained quite undisturbed and all personal belongings were left on board.
The ship's condition was poor – sails were damaged and the glass cover of the ship's compass broken.

When I sent the first mate, Mr Deveau, to the captain's cabin, he noted that navigational instruments were missing and the last log entry was 9 days before. There were ample provisions in the store and no sign that there had been a fire or that any violence had taken place.
David Morehouse (captain)

Over the years, the mystery of the abandoned ship has led to a range of far-fetched explanations: undersea earthquakes, pirates, poison by fumes from the cargo, attack by giant squid, and even alien abduction have all been suggested to explain the desertion of the Mary Celeste.

THE UNSINKABLE TITANIC

— Vessels Rush To Aid Of Sea Colossus —

Floating Palace Thought Unsinkable

World's Most Famous Ship Missing

Entire World Stunned

Carpathia To The Rescue Of Ill-Fated Ship

The deadliest disaster during peacetime took place last night. The largest ship of all time, the Titanic, said to be indestructible, took 1341 lost souls to their watery grave when it struck an iceberg on its maiden voyage to New York.

In the capable hands of the highly experienced Captain Edward Smith, catastrophe crippled the queen of the seas just before midnight, en route to New York.

Ten millionaires were among its illustrious passengers as well as hundreds of emigrants from Europe, seeking a new life in the land of opportunity. Needless to say, the icy depths off the coast of Newfoundland, in equal measure, showed rich and poor no mercy. In an ironic twist of fate, the naval architect, Thomas Andrews, who designed the Titanic, went down with his own creation.

At the time of writing, the Carpathia, responding to mayday calls, has rescued over 700 passengers from lifeboats. God willing, more will be found.

More news will be released as the facts are reliably confirmed. Presently, we are receiving reports, both alarming and reassuring: initial optimism is giving way to despair with the sinister news we have been receiving since midnight.

FACT FILE:
Launched – Belfast, 31st May 1911.
20 lifeboats for a full capacity of 3300 persons.
Maiden voyage – Southampton to New York, 10th April 1912.
2224 passengers and crew.
Captain – Edward Smith.
At 11:40 pm on 14th April 1912 struck iceberg 375 miles south of Newfoundland.

In 1985, using the latest, undersea robotic technology, a joint American-French expedition found the disintegrating hulk of the Titanic. Previous researchers had returned with only tantalising hints of its presence. Led by Dr Robert Ballard, this new team found the wreckage at a depth of over 12,000 feet.

Startled by the very strangeness of the shivering motion, I sprang to the floor... No confusion, no noise of any kind, one could believe no danger imminent. Looking out into the companionway, I saw heads appearing asking questions... All sepulchrally still, no excitement... On either side stand quietly, bravely, the stewards, all equipped with the white, ghostly life-preservers... The awful goodbyes ... brave American men saw us to the lifeboat, made no effort to save themselves, but stepped back on deck. Later they went to an honoured grave.
[Extract from A. Gracie, The Truth About the Titanic (Amberley, 1912)]

NARROW ESCAPE

Hi to all beautiful and intelligent followers of my SUMMER TORTURE blog.

Before today's update, a word of explanation about the slideshow you can see going by above. Mum is hiding because her hair's in a mess. That's Dad doing his admiral bit on the narrowboat he's imprisoned us in this summer. He calls it an 'escape from the humdrum routine of city life'. Next to that is Spider the dog. He can't help being that scruffy. My brother, the evil one, known from now on as Darth, is the one on the right. It's a drawing I did when he was looking his best. Spider is my bodyguard. Chases any vicious ducks threatening to nibble my toes.

We've just taken ages to go through Bath Deep Lock – to get from one level up to a higher level on the Kennet and Avon Canal. Dad says it's 19 feet 5 inches deep. I sat on the roof of the boat. The walls of the lock were slimy but fascinating. Baby frogs, newts and other unidentifiable creatures were clinging to the stone. So now we're leaving busy Bath and heading into the wilderness – not a shop window in sight. I thought I saw a shop through the trees but it could have been a mirage.

Dad keeps telling me stuff to take my mind off civilisation, such as:

- The Kennet and Avon Canal was built around 1800 and took 16 years.
  (So a bit older than Grandad!)
- It fell into disuse when they built the Great Western Railway.
  (Do I have enough money for a train ticket?)
- A few miles ahead is the staircase of 29 locks at Devizes – one after another.
  (My friends, Millie and Radhika, have gone to an Italian villa with an infinity pool!)

(continued on page 4)

We stopped to collect pine cones for a fire to brew up some tea. I hate tea [see previous blogs], but the pine cones smelled nice.

Mum said if Darth and I stopped pestering each other, she might take us on our bikes to a Thai restaurant tomorrow night. Darth isn't going if they don't do chips.

Walking to a visitor centre for an ice cream, they were almost my last moments on Earth, thanks to the reckless steering of a short-sighted, 99-year-old cyclist. Darth was chased by a Canada Goose, who eventually cornered his raspberry and vanilla. When we got back, Dad had got out his guitar. And was playing it. Outside! On the towpath! In public! Spider, being a music-lover, jumped overboard and thrashed around in an adjacent reed bed and howled. (Spider is a menace to wildlife and a destroyer of peace and quiet, though not the only one. The other plays a guitar! Loudly!)

Midnight Blog:
We have survived death by 29 locks. But only just. We went for supper at a nearby pub called 'The Angry Goose'. But Mum is not talking to Dad, I have blisters from turning the windlass*, Darth had to run for his life when he found his old friend, the Canada Goose, waiting for him outside the pub, and Dad is not talking to anybody because he was outvoted on the question of whether we continued on our canal trip to Teddington. That's 107 miles at 4 mph. How many bad-hair days and blisters would that have been? RESULT! That's what I call a NARROW ESCAPE!

Here is my version of the pub sign.
Please leave your comments.

Thank you.
Sacha

VISITORS
002759

Like

* **windlass** is a handle for opening / closing lock gates, and to control water level.

HeadStart primary

Reading Comprehension

YEAR 6

Scaled Score TEST C

ANSWER BOOKLET

Name: ....

Class: ....

Date: ....

Raw Score .... /50

Scaled Score ....

The following questions are about ***THE MYSTERY OF THE MARY CELESTE*** (Page 1)

1. What was the Mary Celeste called to begin with?

   .... 1 mark

2. When was the ship launched?

   .... 1 mark

3. How did the ship come to be referred to as the **Marie** Celeste?

   ....

   .... 1 mark

4. What fictional character is the author, Arthur Conan Doyle, famous for?

   .... 1 mark

5. When was the ship found deserted?

   .... 1 mark

6. **Passengers... abandoned the vessel on the way to Africa.**

   What does **abandoned** mean? **Tick one.**

   left ☐

   destroyed ☐

   joined ☐

   1 mark

Page Total

7 Why do you think the picture has been entitled **The Ghost Ship**?

.... 1 mark

8 Who was able to provide an eyewitness account?

.... 1 mark

9 Write down another word for **falsehoods**.

.... 1 mark

10 What route was the ship following before it was found with no one on board?

.... 1 mark

11 Two things were found undisturbed. What were they?

1. ....

2. .... 2 marks

12 Write down **three** things that were damaged or missing.

1. ....

2. ....

3. .... 2 marks

13 Look at the last paragraph of David Morehouse's account.

He considers what might have caused the ship to be drifting on its own, but he can find no evidence.

Write down **two** of the causes he considers.

1. ....

....

2. ....

....

2 marks

14 Write down **three** of the more far-fetched explanations for the mystery of the Mary Celeste.

1. ....

2. ....

3. ....

2 marks

End of questions about
THE MYSTERY OF THE MARY CELESTE

The following questions are about ***THE UNSINKABLE TITANIC*** (Page 2)

1. What was the name of the ship that rushed to the scene to save as many passengers of the Titanic as possible?

   ....

   1 mark

2. Write down a metaphor used in the newspaper report to describe the Titanic.

   ....

   1 mark

3. Where was the Titanic going?

   ....

   1 mark

4. How does the first paragraph of the newspaper article describe the fate of those who drowned?

   ....

   1 mark

5. Write down an example from the newspaper of alliteration.

   ....

   1 mark

6. Who are the two types of passenger described by the newspaper?

   1. ....

   ....

   2. ....

   ....

   2 marks

7 **'... the icy depths ... in equal measure, showed rich and poor no mercy.'** Write this in your own words.

....

....

.... 1 mark

8 Where did the collision take place?

.... 1 mark

9 Who was Thomas Andrews?

....

.... 1 mark

10 **Tick** the boxes according to whether the following statements are **facts** or **opinions**.

statement	fact	opinion
The Carpathia has rescued over 700 passengers from lifeboats .		
More news will be released as the facts are reliably confirmed.		
We are receiving conflicting reports, both alarming and reassuring.		

2 marks

11 In 1985, how did Dr Robert Ballard's expedition manage to find the sunken ship?

.... 1 mark

12 The **'team found the wreckage at a depth of 12,000 feet'.**

What other phrase is used to describe what remained of the ship?

.... 1 mark

13 Look at the text beginning: **'Startled by the very strangeness . . .'**

What kind of text is this?

.... 1 mark

14 In arriving at your answer to **question 13**, what clues in the text did you consider? Write down **two** clues.

1. ....

2. .... 2 marks

15 How does the writer of the final section describe the first signs of hitting an iceberg?

.... 1 mark

16 **Circle** a word that means the same as **companionway**.

friendship group | corridor | lifeboat

1 mark

17 The final section was written by a woman. How can you tell?

....

.... 1 mark

End of questions about
THE UNSINKABLE TITANIC

The following questions are about ***NARROW ESCAPE*** (Page 3 - 4)

1. Why isn't there a photograph of Mum?

   .... 1 mark

2. Sacha calls her blog **SUMMER TORTURE**. In the 1st paragraph, what phrase supports her choice of title?

   .... 1 mark

3. What is the purpose of a canal lock?

   .... 1 mark

4. Sacha suggests she is not happy about leaving the city of Bath. Why is she not happy?

   ....

   .... 1 mark

5. What was the effect on the canal system of building the railways?

   .... 1 mark

6. Why has Sacha mentioned her friends, Millie and Radhika, in brackets with an exclamation mark?

   .... 1 mark

Page Total

7 Choose a word that is similar in meaning to **adjacent**.

distant | separate | neighbouring

1 mark

8 When Sacha says that Spider is a **destroyer of peace and quiet, though not the only one**, who else does she have in mind?

....

1 mark

9 What town has the family reached when Sacha writes her Midnight Blog?

....

1 mark

10 There are at least **two** things we know Darth likes to eat. What are they?

1. ....

2. ....

1 mark

11 Why did Darth have to run for his life outside The Angry Goose?

....

1 mark

12 Why is Sacha relieved she doesn't have to travel the 107 miles to Teddington?

....

....

1 mark

End of questions about
NARROW ESCAPE

End of TEST C

HeadStart
primary

YEAR 6

Reading Comprehension

ANSWERS & MARK SCHEME

Scaled Score TESTS A, B & C

Once a test has been marked, a raw score out of 50 can be awarded.
This score should then be converted to a scaled score using the conversion charts in the digital version.

The table below can then be used to identify progress against one of the 6 stages. (See notes in the digital version for further information.)

Year 6

NB: The stage boundaries and 3 'standards' in the table below are intended as a guide to children's progress. They should not be interpreted in the same way as a scaled score of 100 is used as 'standard met' in KS1 and KS2 SATs.

Scaled Score	Stage	
0 - 75	Emerging	Working towards the expected standard
76 - 95	Developing	
96 - 100	Progressing	Working within the expected standard
101 - 112	Secure	
113 - 122	Exceeding	Working above the expected standard
123 +	Exceeding with greater depth	

The assessments are intended to be used by teachers as a tool to support their professional judgement. The table above should be used only as a guide to achievement and progress. This data should always be used in conjunction with ongoing teacher assessment.

Content domain

The text and table below are taken directly from the 'Key Stage 2 English reading test framework'. This document is used by test designers to create the Key Stage 2 SAT.

The appropriate 'domains' are identified in the following HeadStart mark scheme.

Key stage 2 English reading test framework **7**

4. Content domain

The content domain sets out the relevant elements from the national curriculum programme of study (2014) for English at key stage 2 that are assessed in the English reading test. The tests will, over time, sample from each area of the content domain.

The key stage 2 English reading tests will focus on the comprehension elements of the national curriculum.

Table 2 shows the content domain, which sets out how elements of the curriculum will be defined for test development purposes.

Table 2: Content domain relating to questions

Content domain reference	
2a	give / explain the meaning of words in context
2b	retrieve and record information / identify key details from fiction and non-fiction
2c	summarise main ideas from more than one paragraph
2d	make inferences from the text / explain and justify inferences with evidence from the text
2e	predict what might happen from details stated and implied
2f	identify / explain how information / narrative content is related and contributes to meaning as a whole
2g	identify / explain how meaning is enhanced through choice of words and phrases
2h	make comparisons within the text

Buffalo Bill's Wild West			
No.	**Answers and Mark Scheme**	**Domain**	**Marks**
1	Iowa = 1 mark Kansas = 1 mark	2b	2
2	14 (years old)	2b	1
3	10 days	2b	1
4	American Civil War = 1 mark Plains Wars = 1 mark	2b	2
5	scout	2b	1
6	He hunted buffalo to provide food for the army.	2b	1
7	trapper / goldminer / wagon-master / stagecoach driver / hotel manager **[Any three correct answers for 2 marks. Any two correct answers for 1 mark.]**	2b	2
8	1883	2b	1
9	His show toured the country. / It was a massively popular attraction.	2d	1
10	sharp-shooting by Annie Oakley = 1 mark re-enactments of the Pony Express = 1 mark rodeo skills = 1 mark rescue of white settlers (wagon trains) under attack by Native Americans = 1 mark	2b	3
11	Lakota / Sioux	2b	1
12	He respected the Native Americans. = 1 mark He supported the rights of Native Americans. = 1 mark He provided employment to improve their lives. = 1 mark He blamed the government for broken promises and treaties. = 1 mark **[Award 1 mark for each correct answer up to a maximum of 3 marks.]**	2b	3
13	Queen Victoria's jubilee (50 years on the throne)	2b	1
14	It provides the dates of the key moments in his life.	2f	1
15	It provides basic information about when he was alive, as well as an image of the man.	2f	1

The Industrial Revolution			
No.	**Answers and Mark Scheme**	**Domain**	**Marks**
1	Britain changed from a rural society (working on a farm and / or at home) to the most advanced industrialised country in the world. = 2 marks	2b	2
2	mainly	2a	1
3	cottage industries	2b	1
4	rich - had electric lights, rode in cars poor - lived in a single room, worked in factories **[Award 2 marks for all four correct answers. Award 1 mark for any two, or three correct answers.]**	2h	2
5	camera	2d	1
6	poor child working in a factory	2d	1
7	the use of 'we'	2d	1
8	He wasn't worried about speaking his mind.	2a	1
9	crime = 1 mark disease = 1 mark	2b	2
10	When Dickens was 12, his father went to prison. = 1 mark He had to work in a (dirty, noisy and dangerous) factory. = 1 mark	2d	2
11	1837	2d	1
12	He spends some time in a workhouse. = 1 mark He becomes a member of a criminal gang / and learns to be a pickpocket. = 1 mark	2b	2

Let Them Eat Cake

No.	Answers and Mark Scheme	Domain	Marks
1	**Any two from these examples:** like / wanna know why / You know / Well... did it? / D'you know	2f	1
2	upside-down	2a	1
3	Trying to sleep is the hardest bit.	2c	1
4	Tarte Tatin	2b	1
5	He thinks he'll have an advantage [=1 mark] by making a cake that has the same name as the school and that this will impress the judges. [= 1 mark]	2d	2
6	Sophie and Sammy	2h	1
7	He ate the almonds.	2e	1
8	The reader is drawn into what feels like a one-to-one conversation (eliciting empathy).	2f	1
9	There might be nothing left. / They might leave a few crumbs behind.	2d	1
10	Kira - she says, 'She'll be really pleased when I tell her the results.'	2d	1

TOTAL	50

The Wildlife-Friendly Garden			
No.	**Answers and Mark Scheme**	**Domain**	**Marks**
1	Mrs Brown	2d	1
2	slightly	2a	1
3	**Any two of the following (maximum 2 marks):** Same for people observing pond life habitat. / In talks with local garden centre for free plants past their best. / Might Yr 5 make bird boxes - DT project? / Also bird feeders? / Miss Flint to set up bird-box webcam.	2f	2
4	Children might eat holly berries.	2d	1
5	They would be safe from predators.	2d	1
6	gravel placed at front edge of the pond	2a	1
7	attract insects / attract birds that eat insects / small mammals eat elderberries **[Award 2 marks for all three correct answers. Award 1 mark for any two correct answers.]**	2b	2
8	hedgehogs, solitary bees and other insects	2b	1
9	elder, holly	2b	1
10	Its nectar attracts butterflies.	2b	1
11	Baby birds hatching and growing (or similar)	2d	1
12	Jonah Eve	2d	1
13	**Award 1 mark for an appropriate answer. Suggested examples:** His parents don't know yet. / His parents never volunteer. / His parents always volunteer. / Baz is very / surprisingly keen to contribute to the development of the garden.	2d	1
14	refill	2a	1
15	**One mark for each of the following correct answers up to a total of 3 marks:** logs for the insect hotel / paving for the path / large natural rocks for the pond.	2b	3
16	**Award 1 mark for each correct answer up to a total of 3 marks:** science - studying habitats / life cycles DT - making bird boxes and feeders English - writing updates for the school newsletter art - drawing plants and wildlife	2d	3

The Artist's Garden			
No.	**Answers and Mark Scheme**	**Domain**	**Marks**
1	Either 'FAQs', 'Check Availability' button, or customer reviews	2f	1
2	personal guide	2d	1
3	Some visitors take longer to look at things.	2d	1
4	Yes	2b	1
5	Award 1 mark for an answer based on the stated rule that visitors are not allowed to have picnics.	2e	1
6	**One mark for each of the following correct answers up to a total of 3 marks:** glorious garden / colourful flowerbeds / beauty of the climbing plants / joyful sight of the water-lily pond	2g	3
7	opinion - fact - opinion - opinion **[Award 2 marks for all four correct answers. Award 1 mark for any two or three correct answers.]**	2g	2
8	They are very good at gardening.	2a	1
9	**Stand** and **admire** are imperative verbs.	2f	1
10	He painted the same landscape in different light at different times of the day.	2b	1
11	FAQs - 'Children must remain calm and respect the premises and other visitors.' = 1 mark Review - 'not the place for two lively six-year-olds.' = 1 mark	2b	2
12	whisk you away from the hubbub of Paris / delve into the past	2h	1
13	memorable	2a	1

Micro-organisms			
No.	**Answers and Mark Scheme**	**Domain**	**Marks**
1	vunerable	2a	1
2	doctor	2b	1
3	He witnessed soldiers dying from simple infections.	2d	1
4	To kill the germs. = 1 mark To prevent disease in any patient operated upon. = 1 mark	2d	2
5	Alexander Fleming	2d	1
6	Soldiers were dying of infection.	2c	1
7	Scutari (in the Crimea)	2b	1
8	Louis Pasteur	2h	1
9	similar to the blue mould that grows on bread	2b	1
10	basic hygiene + fresh food	2b	1

TOTAL	50

The Mystery of the Mary Celeste			
No.	**Answers and Mark Scheme**	**Domain**	**Marks**
1	Amazon	2b	1
2	1861	2b	1
3	Arthur Conan Doyle wrote a story featuring a ship called the Marie Celeste.	2b	1
4	Sherlock Holmes	2b	1
5	4th December, 1872	2b	1
6	left	2a	1
7	It was found sailing on its own without a crew.	2d	1
8	David Morehouse	2b	1
9	lies	2a	1
10	New York to Genoa	2b	1
11	its cargo = 1 mark all personal belongings = 1 mark	2b	2
12	ship's compass / sails / lifeboats / navigational instruments **[Award 2 marks for any three correct answers; 1 mark for any two correct answers.]**	2b	2
13	**Award 1 mark for each correct answer, up to a total of 2:** those on board had run out of food / fire / violence	2d	2
14	undersea earthquakes / pirates / poison by fumes from the cargo / attack by giant squid / alien abduction **[Award 2 marks for three correct answers; 1 mark for two correct answers.]**	2b	2

The Unsinkable Titanic			
No.	**Answers and Mark Scheme**	**Domain**	**Marks**
1	Carpathia	2b	1
2	**Award 1 mark for any of the following:** sea colossus / floating palace / queen of the seas	2g	1
3	New York	2b	1
4	took 1341 lost souls to their watery grave	2b	1
5	**Award 1 mark for any of the following:** deadliest disaster / catastrophe crippled the queen	2g	1
6	ten millionaires were among its illustrious passengers = 1 hundreds of emigrants from Europe seeking a new life = 1	2b	2
7	Example: It didn't matter how rich or poor the passengers were, they still died in the freezing seas. / The sea didn't distinguish between millionaires and poor emigrants.	2a	1
8	off the coast of Newfoundland / 375 miles south of Newfoundland	2b	1
9	the naval architect who designed the Titanic (and went down with the ship)	2d	1
10	fact - fact - opinion **[Award 1 mark for two correct.]**	2b	2
11	It used the latest, undersea robot technology.	2b	1
12	disintegrating hulk	2g	1
13	autobiography (accept 'diary')	2f	1
14	**Award 2 marks for any two of the following correct answers; 1 mark for one correct answer.** personal experience / comments / feelings / past tense / chronology of events / 1st person	2f	2
15	strangeness of the shivering motion	2g	1
16	corridor	2a	1
17	**Award 1 mark for either of the following:** She describes the 'brave American men' as if they were helping her into a lifeboat. Women (and children) were saved first.	2d	1

Narrow Escape

No.	Answers and Mark Scheme	Domain	Marks
1	Her hair's in a mess.	2b	1
2	the narrowboat he's imprisioned us in	2h	1
3	It takes canal boats from one level up to a higher level.	2b	1
4	She is leaving the shops behind.	2d	1
5	The canal(s) fell into disuse.	2b	1
6	She would prefer to be with them and not with her family on a narrowboat holiday.	2d	1
7	neighbouring	2a	1
8	Dad / her father	2f	1
9	Devizes	2d	1
10	chips + ice cream	2b	1
11	The Canada Goose was after him.	2b	1
12	She won't have to suffer any more bad-hair days and / or blisters.	2d	1

TOTAL	50

PLEASE NOTE:

The digital version also contains the book and tests filed separately for printing. A full answer version and colour digital versions of the book and tests are also included.

The raw score/scaled score conversion charts are also supplied.

PLEASE NOTE:

The digital version also contains the book and tests filed separately for printing. A full answer version and colour digital versions of the book and tests are also included.

The raw score/scaled score conversion charts are also supplied.